POSITIVE INFLUENCE

How to Lead Your World

A whole-person developmental approach for leaders

GRANT D. FAIRLEY

A POSITIVE INFLUENCE
in MINDSOR !

POSITIVE INFLUENCE
How to Lead Your World

A whole-person developmental approach for leaders

All rights reserved. No part of this book may be reproduced in any form or by any electronic or mechanical means, including information storage and retrieval systems, without permission in writing from the publisher, except by a reviewer, who may quote brief passages in a review.

Published By: Silverwoods Publishing
www.silverwoods-publishing.com

ISBN 978-1-897202-15-9
Cover Design by Artist's Tree
Cover Photo – logoboom/bigstock.com

All rights reserved.
Printed in the United States of America
First Edition
© 2013 Silverwoods Publishing

DEDICATION

This book is dedicated to all who are willing to answer the call to serve as a leader.

IN MEMORIAM

This book is in memory of my friend Kevin Dunsmuir. He, along with his wife Jennifer and two of their teenage children, Robert and Cameron, died tragically in a house fire this year.

Our prayers continue for their surviving son David and the family and friends who experienced this terrible loss.

We walked many dark and bright roads together, my friend. Too soon have you left our road. We are comforted in knowing that you all have arrived at a better place now.

TABLE OF CONTENTS

Dedication v
In Memoriam vii
Introduction..xiii
Acknowledgments xv

A Positive Influence..1
A Center of Influence..5
Following the Leader 9
Who Am I? 13
Conductors and Captains...19
Exploring the Wilderness 23
What Time Is It? 27
The Red Mist 31
Finding Your Center...35
The Situation Room...39
Investing in You 43
Sprints and Marathons 45
The Real Deal 49
The Return of the King..53

The Heart of the Leader 55

Decisions 59

I Doubt It! 63

Creating Your Biography 67

Oranges and Bananas 71

Pen or Pencil 75

Arts and Sciences 79

The Lighthouse and the Leader 83

Who Are They? 89

Your Inheritance 93

Boo! 97

Shots Fired 99

Shooting the Rapids 103

Hail to the Chiefs 107

Did You Bring the Playbook? 111

Positive Persuasion 113

Bridges 117

On the Boil and on the Wobble 121

Knowing Your Motto 125

Firefighting 127

Sitting on the Bench 131

The One and the Many 135

Cheers 139

On a Swing or on Fire? 143

Playing a Friendly 147

Check, Please! 151

The Power to Forgive 155

Breaking the Ice 159

Tell Me a Story 165

Stage Coach 169

Magic Wands and Magic Lamps 173
Robes and Crowns 177
The Human Condition 181
3-D Leaders 185
Exit Stage Right 189
It's Been an Honor 193
Developing Old Friends 197
Sail On 201
The Executive Coach 203
Choosing an Executive Coach 207
Speak to Be Heard 211

Useful Links and Contacts 217
For Further Investigation 221
Postscript 223
About the Author 227

INTRODUCTION

Many of the topics I share during a seminar trigger more questions and interactions than there is time to address after the session. When the topic relates to leadership, I always wish I had more time to follow up since I have a great respect for those willing to lead. Some of the people at the seminars come to me for professional development in my role as an executive coach. There we can tailor the content to the real-life dramas that are going on with the leader in their life as an executive or top salesperson. This book allows me to share beyond the coaching process and the seminars some of what I think is helpful for all leaders to know.

I have the privilege of working with women and men in all areas of business, government, education, community leadership and various professions. I continue to learn from each one as I walk with them on their journey.

There are many excellent leadership books out there. This is my contribution of a few of the big ideas that seem to be most helpful in the seminars and coaching.

My goal was to make this accessible for a leader at any stage. I especially hope that new and prospective leaders will have a chance to read this book in preparation for their responsibilities.

Thank you for taking the time to read this book. I look forward to your feedback. Please feel free to contact me at fairley@strategic-seminars.com.

ACKNOWLEDGMENTS

This was one of those projects that has been impatient with me. While I have been busy working on other assignments and opportunities, this book has regularly cleared its throat so that I would not forget that it, too, was waiting for my attention.

It was not that I was avoiding this one. It is a useful topic and one that captures much of what I do in my coaching life. It just seemed to be postponed a number of times until now.

With apologies to the book for delaying its release (feel better now?), I would like to acknowledge the many others who made this book possible.

I owe a debt to the many people who modeled leadership to me in my youth and adult life. Some went the extra mile to mentor my leadership. I also had the privilege of studying leadership and personal development at Wheaton College near Chicago. It is a college that had a great history of producing leaders in a wide range of disciplines in the United States and around the world. The kind of leadership that was taught and modeled there was a whole-person approach. There we were taught an understanding of leadership as an opportunity to serve, not to rule.

Throughout my life, it has been my good fortune to meet many interesting leaders. From each one I have observed and learned to prepare myself as a leader. I recognized early on that each leader was unique, even when they followed a similar method. That was very helpful.

In the many leadership positions where I had the privilege to serve, I learned from all those who were part of those teams as leaders and colleagues. Most were very patient and tolerant of my leadership successes and failures. I am grateful to the many who continue to be friends from those varied chapters in my story when it was my turn to lead.

Encouragement from an understanding spouse is an essential ingredient in any writing project. My enchanting wife Cari has generously listened to me during the times when this project excited me and through other times when I wished it would just go away. Throughout, she gave me the support I needed to keep on keeping on with this book.

There are also some who regularly urge me to finish those books I have begun. Friends and colleagues like Dr. Blair Lamb, Mike Lanthier and Andras Rameshwar always have an encouraging word. Thank you!

Among the many leaders I have known who have had a significant impact on my life and thinking at different stages of my life are: Maurice Muller, Grant Steidl, Russ Skaling, James Sparks, James Sparrow, Jair Hall, Fred Carlson, Jerry Dimmick, James Rendle, Murray Knights, Roy Lawson, Paul Hadley, Walter Gast, Bruce Neal, Gary Carter, Nicholas Wester, Maurice Cullity, Ward Pipher, Peter Jarvis, Stuart Fickett, Bryce Taylor, Floyd McKee, David Garshowitz, Dr. Larry Komer, Ross Downing, Dr. George Bell, Ron McKerlie, Bill Masson and Ted Roberts.

From Wheaton College, professors and leaders especially significant to me were: Norman Ericson, Hudson Armerding, Howard Newsom, Rodney McKean, James McCue, Will Norton, Sam Shellhammer, Alan Johnson, Evan Welsh, William Pollard, and Gerald Hawthorne.

From the team at Silverwoods Publishing, my transcriptionist, Paige Alverez, patiently converted many hours of speech into text for me. Jeny Lyn Ruelo once again did great work in laying out the book. The cover design was by my wife Cari, and my daughter Emma prepared the cover layout. Paul Archie Teleron was very helpful in handling our digital images.

Excellent editing by David Moadel once again improved the clarity of the book. Gwen Giudici has been our web expert to improve the digital home of the coaching and seminar websites.

"A positive attitude will kindle the hearts of good people to do great things."

Grant D. Fairley

A POSITIVE INFLUENCE

As an executive coach, my role is to provide professional development to executives and leaders. Building on their current experience, we work together to add additional tools to their leadership. I am there to encourage and challenge them as leaders. As a mentor or colleague, I provide a way for leaders to step outside the everyday challenges to process what is going on.

We concentrate on who the leader is with all the complexities of their strengths, weaknesses, passions, talents, education, experiences, failures and successes. It is a process of personal development applied to the workplace.

My goal is a simple one: Develop effective, sustainable and renewable leaders.

To be effective as a leader, we believe that a person has to be able to apply what is needed when it is needed to the opportunity they have to be the leader.

Sustainable leadership means that a person is not a flash in the pan or someone who is only able to lead for a short term before their effectiveness fades. Instead, with a whole-person focus, they will understand how to not just sprint but do the leadership marathon as well.

Renewable leaders are able to understand how to continue to learn and grow rather than become stuck in a method or mindset that is inflexible.

Some leaders come to me on their own initiative. After one of my seminars on leadership or related topics, executives often connect to spend some time applying the concepts to them personally. Many come by referral. Occasionally, they have been encouraged to meet at the recommendation of their human resources or employment relations team to strengthen their leadership.

How long they have served in leadership is also varied. Some are newly appointed. Others have a great deal of experience. Executives may be facing a fierce storm that has put their position in jeopardy. Others are meeting for a routine tune-up to ensure that all continues to go well. On some occasions, it is a leader who has just achieved a major result that has been long in coming. They now have to deal with leadership after a major accomplishment.

The people I meet are from large and small corporations, government, law, education, entrepreneurs and community organizations.

While most are executives, some are sales leaders who face their own pressures to perform and achieve results. They look for strategies and tactics to help them at work and in the larger context of their life.

As with most people who have the opportunity to work with executives, it is always fascinating. These are all interesting people doing interesting work. The variety of fields from which they come along with the wide age range means that my time with them is always an adventure.

There are many styles of leadership and many different schools of thought on how to get results. What you will see in the course of this book is a philosophy of leadership that is based neither on control nor on a passive arm's-length style. As the title of the book suggests, my view is that the best leadership happens by leaders being a positive influence. This book is about how to be an influential leader whether you are leading a government, a large corporation or a small group at work or in your community.

Influence is an approach that I believe is most consistent with best practices for a leader producing the best long-term outcomes. There certainly are short-term advantages to many other leadership styles. However, leaders who truly make a difference do so from their personal strengths, talents and gifts being used to the benefit of their team, their customers and their other stakeholders.

Do you want to be an effective leader? Be a positive influence.

A CENTER OF INFLUENCE

As children, we have all enjoyed tossing a pebble into a pond. The splash is followed by those mystical rings that ripple out from the center. Like messengers, these waves carry the impact of that pebble in all directions until they reach a shoreline or gradually fade out of view. We soon learn that the larger the rock we throw into the pond, the greater the splash and the rings that radiate out.

Those who make the greatest difference in their world are each a center of positive influence. Like the stone above, they have an ongoing effect reaching far beyond where they are. In this book, we will consider not only how to be influential but how to be a positive influence wherever you are.

Images, pictures and metaphors help us move beyond the clinical terminology of management. It allows us to get to the essence of leadership – the whole person. It is not enough to "know" what it means to be a leader; you have to "be" the leader. Effective leaders bring all aspects of their being to the challenge of guiding, mentoring and making decisions with their team. As we consider leadership in this book, we will consider who the various parts of "who" you are come into play in making you an effective leader.

These centers of influence can be in business, government, community, the arts, education or even in a family. They do more than just perform their tasks or fulfill their obligations.

People who have mastered the ability to make a difference in their world understood who they are as well as what they can do. Then they do it – again and again and again.

The impact they have begins first with those closest to them. Then, as they develop, their influence is felt further and further away. As they become more and more substantial in who they are and what they are doing, their splash of influence grows, extending the waves that flow out from their lives.

The positive influencers are the best in their profession. They are most effective people in business, the top people in sales, and the ones who can bring a community together. In education, they are the educators who inspire their students. As people of faith, they make time for the "least of these" in their circle. As artists, their creativity is channeled to enchant others. In a family, they are the family member who is always there for the near and distant relative.

Centers of influence always contrast with a controlling force. We have all experienced people who use force, threat and domination to control others to achieve their ends. These controllers can divide and conquer. Their most useful tool is fear. They can defeat others, but they are never an influence. Ultimately, people resent and reject those who lead by force and intimidation no matter how much control they exert for a time.

The people who make a lasting difference in their world choose influence rather than force. The tool that they use most is trust. To influence is to recognize the value of a choice. It is an invitation to see or experience something that together could create a positive outcome. To force is to make the choice for someone else and to exert your will over others to serve your chosen end result.

In the following chapters, we will explore what makes someone a center of influence. We will also show you how to become a positive influence in your world. For those of you who already are making ripples, you will learn how to make waves instead by becoming a more substantial and effective person no matter who you are, where you live or what you want to do.

So pick up a pebble in your mind's eye and give it a toss.

FOLLOWING THE LEADER

Remember when you were a kid playing "follow the leader"? That was a great game. You could take turns being the leader and then a follower. The leader would act, walk, skip or jump in a certain way. Each would imitate her or him. As a team, off you would go. It was not very complicated, and it sure was a lot of fun. Everyone wanted their turn as the leader.

Well, a funny thing happens as you get older: You may not be as excited about the prospect of being the leader. Yet if you are like most people, eventually somewhere in your life, you are going to be called upon to be the leader. Maybe that has just happened to you. Someone in your group at the company or your charitable organization has come up to you and said, "We really need you to help us with our group. Can you help lead us?" You are faced with the same kinds of thing that happen to anybody in any leadership situation anywhere in the world.

Much of the decision-making process depends the personality of your group as well as your own personality. Groups are organic. They do have their own identity, no matter how diverse the members are. That identity may morph over time as members of the group and their leaders change. However, at any particular time, you should recognize the personality traits of the group as well as the leader. As a leader, you will be involved with the shaping of the group's identity and personality. Just as there are attributes that make you *you,* your group is *that* particular group.

When you are called to lead, ensure that you understand what is being asked of you. In some cases, this is defined for you because it is part of an agreement that you are going to a particular position with certain criteria that have already been documented. You will begin a set of duties or responsibilities.

In other cases, your leadership might be required to fix a problem. It could be a management problem or a new direction for the company. You might be in a community organization that is just starting up in response to some need that exists. You may not know what the role is going to be precisely. You are not going to know all of the details. Sometimes you will leading the team on an adventure with no real map given to you except a challenge to make it better or more profitable. The "where" of your leadership is going to be developed over time.

Whatever your leadership challenge is, it helps to have a sense of purpose. You have to have a full understanding of the way ahead, but it will go a long way if you can choose to lead. Making leadership your purpose is powerful if it is not your preference to be the leader.

You may be in a situation where there is no choice; maybe it is part of your job. From time to time you are asked to take on this extra responsibility, and you look at it and say, "I do not really have a choice here. I need to do it because it is part of my job," or, "If I do not do this, then it is going to really hurt me in my potential in the company or my satisfaction with the job." Those kinds of decisions are always there. Still, to the degree possible, if you can, start any leadership position with a sense of purpose. It is a time to say, "I will." If it something that you just do not believe that you can or should do, be just as quick to say, "I will not." That may have negative consequences, but it might still be the correct decision for you. Be sure that it is not just a question of your comfort zone. Growing is uncomfortable but necessary for a fulfilling life. If the opportunity really is something that you should not do, then declare it and stick to your convictions.

If you are going to be an effective leader, it is useful to think about what it means to follow. We have all been in situations where we followed someone who was a terrible leader. Think back to those experiences – we may not need to make the same mistakes that they did. As a leader, it is helpful to think of ourselves as followers first before we think of ourselves as the leader.

What is it like as a member of that community organization, church, business, or team? What does it feel like to be one of those team members? What are their needs? What are the opportunities they hope to experience?

All of those who are part of your team will be very important to the success of your group. As an effective leader, you want to accomplish the tasks but you also want to champion the team experience. Give these other people in your group an experience that they could take and use again. They should be able to replicate the great things that you have done together in other contexts.

Do that and they will want to play follow the leader with you at the head of the line anytime!

WHO AM I?

Down through the ages, a major subject that philosophers, poets, theologians, playwrights and bards – those early self-help gurus – explored the questions: Who are we? What does it mean to be "me" in a wide world of people? Great leaders know who they are.

In our earliest days, we think of our identity as our first name: "I am Richard." Later we connect our last name and the immediate family attached to that relationship: "I am Richard Vaughn. I am Richard Vaughn, son of Patrick and Louise Vaughn. I am the brother of Laura Vaughn." So our tangled web of relationships and connections to family members near and far emerges. Then we add the perspective of time as we begin to understand that there were generations of our family who came before "me" in this world. Our definition begins to take shape, confirming both what is the same about us as family and how I am unique or different despite all of the similarities.

The journey to understand who we are is a lifelong project. What do we like or dislike? What do we care about? What do we avoid? It is journey that takes a lifetime because we are constantly changing as well. Through the passages of life that all human beings experience, we will see life, and therefore ourselves, differently as the decades pass. We will develop this aspect later on in the book.

However, in spite of all the changes and lessons to learn, there are some elements of our personality that take shape early on and largely continue with us. Even though we are all unique as individuals, our personality does have some characteristics that are common to other groups of people in our world. It is part of our nature to want to sort out where we belong while at the same time keeping our individuality.

There are many tests, studies and methods to help us identify our basic "personality type" that helps us understand ourselves better. These have existed classically in four groups that go back to ancient times with the Greek physician Hippocrates who identified them as "humors" that he related to the blood. His four humors were melancholic, phlegmatic, sanguine and choleric. Other ancients looked at temperaments as the four elements of earth, water, air and fire.

Many have considered this down through the ages, especially in the fields of philosophy, theology and psychology.

Archetypes have been around in philosophy for millennia going back to the time of Plato. This is a way of sorting the arche- (first, top or beginning) types (patterns) of people in the world. The desire (or need?) to sort people into types comes from a wish to understand and interact with others effectively. As we gain experience, we encounter new people where we conclude that we have seen someone who acted like this before. We then draw from our experiences from previous relationships to help us with the new. We understand that no two people are identical in personality but our ability to generalize and learn is part of our socialization skill set. As we get to know someone better, we fine-tune our interactions to take into account the nuances and individuality we experience with the person. In most cases, there is not a perfect match between an archetype and an individual but there is often one archetype that seems more evident than others.

There are many lists of archetypes with characteristics for each one. Swiss psychiatrist Carl Jung had one of the early lists that have formed the basis of many other ways to sort out the personalities. The 12 Common

Archetypes referenced by Carl Golden and also found in books by Carol S. Pearson are: the Ruler, the Magician, the Hero, the Sage, the Explorer, the Rebel, the Lover, the Creator, the Jester, the Innocent, the Orphan/Regular Person and the Caregiver. Which of these types of personalities connect with how you see yourself? Would friends and family agree or would they see a different title for you? Do you feel like you are a blend of two of these archetypes?

All of this relates to the development and understanding of our "personal mythology" where we live our lives in ways that reflect how we see ourselves. Myth, in this context, is not something that is not true. Instead, it is a way of seeing a story from outside of ourselves. Like all great myths, the process of stepping back allows us to see truths about the story that are difficult to recognize while we are in the middle of the action. It is like the difference between writing your autobiography and someone writing your biography.

Some consider their "personal mythology" to be given to them, much like our DNA. That can flow from the long history of our ancestors who continue to echo in our own time though they are long gone. Others view each life having a special purpose for which we have been specially equipped. This relates to our understanding of being gifted, talented or in some way "purposed" to do or become who we become. It connects to a perspective that life is not just a random accident of nature but that there is a reason why we are here. This is particularly true of those who see a spiritual significance in our life purpose.

Others believe that we begin as a tabula rasa (blank slate) with the full range of possibilities to be discovered and written as our story. Here, too, there is a wide range of viewpoints. Some believe that we become a product of our environment and upbringing. Others believe that it is always a matter of choices made by the individual.

This is not far from the old debate of "nature or nurture" that asks whether we are the product of our genes or our upbringing and experiences. Like most great debates, there is likely truth on both sides.

It does matter how we see ourselves, as this does inform our thinking as we deal with life events. Do we interpret negative events as normal and random? Do they become a challenge for us to overcome? Are the good times an affirmation of a life well lived, or is it all chance? Great leaders have sorted this out for themselves. Some have believed that they lived a purposed life. Others believe it to be a life that just worked out the way it did by the chances taken or neglected. Recognizing your personal mythology is highly valuable.

In our times, a number of helpful tests have been developed to provide a standardized way to gain insight into the question of our identity and personality. Two of the most popular tests today are the Myers-Briggs Type Indicator (MBTI®) and the DISC® assessment.

The DISC® concepts were created by psychologist William Marston in the 1920s and were formalized into tests and profiles in the 1950s. The assessment sorts people primarily into Dominance, Inducement (or sometimes called Influencer,) Submission (or Steadiness,) and Compliance (or Caution or Conscientiousness) as the basic personality types.

Myers-Briggs was created by a mother-daughter combination around WWII based on their study of psychiatrist Carl Jung. It was in the 1960s that the test became more popular. It measures where each person fits on a range of four aspects of personality such as whether one is more of an extrovert vs. introvert, sensing vs. intuition, thinking vs. feeling, and judging vs. perception. People then can identify themselves with a four-letter descriptor that reflects where they would fit on that grid of 16 combinations.

There are many other types of tests out there, as well. The sorting hat from Harry Potter is not usually available, but let me tell you about my favorite one that is just as magical.

Psycho-Geometrics® was recommended to me by my brother after he attend a corporate seminar at his company in the early 1990s. I received a copy of the book. It was not only thoughtful, well-written and entertaining, but was also very easy to apply. I knew right away that I was reading something very special.

It was created by my friend Dr. Susan Dellinger, who used her skills as a communications specialist to design an incredibly intuitive yet accurate tool. It instantly identifies our communication style. The insight she had was to use the most common shapes of a circle, triangle, box, rectangle and squiggly line. Once identified, she created very helpful descriptions that people usually find affirms their gut decision. Like a cool magic trick, you want to know how she did it. This is one of the best ways to explore your communication styles that are so important to effective leadership. If you have never heard Susan speak, read the book or taken the Psycho-Geometrics® test, you are in for a great "a-ha!" moment.

If you have yet to acquire an understanding what communication style you use, I would recommend that you take the online or written Psycho-Geometrics® at www.psychogeometrics.com. Enter the discount code Wheaton and receive a discount on the test.

Your human resources department may have these or other tests available to explore your personality and styles of communication or leadership.

It will surprise you how much fun you can have peering into these tests that act as mirrors of who we are. As a leader, it will help you on the journey to better understand that question: "Who am I?"

CONDUCTORS AND CAPTAINS

When it comes to leadership styles and approaches, we use a number of different models to get people to think about how they lead. One model I would like you to look at would be the difference between a old-time train conductor and a ship's captain plying the high seas generations ago.

These are two different kinds of roles; both are leaders, yet the kind of leadership they can provide can be very different due to the nature of their assignment.

If you think about the conductor of the train, the conductor has a number of different tasks. Some of these assignments are quite visible, such as on a passenger train when the conductor walks through the train and is supervising as the "face" of the train. Yet, they also have some hidden roles that people do not see. Conductors are the ones who receive the assignments from the head office for the train and its crew. The conductor is responsible for the general running of the freight or passenger train. They are the authority on the train if something is to be decided in an emergency or for other unexpected events requiring decisions along the way. The conductor is the person in charge of the crew, providing leadership on a number of different levels.

The train is operating on a series of tracks. These tracks are laid down, and the conductor is the one responsible for getting the train from A to B and B to C and so on. The essential task is to arrive safely and on time. The conductor's job is really to coordinate with the engineer and with the others who are involved in the maintenance and the function of the train to make the train operate smoothly and to have minimal problems as the train moves from station to station. When you think about the role of the conductor and the nature of trains, it really is following a path that has been laid out.

The people who adopt the conductor style of management tend to be those leaders who like to know where they are going and know the stops along the way. They have a clear sense of function, role, and responsibility. The role follows the routines that are highly established and that everyone understands. They know the amount of time expected and the decisions necessary to minimize the variables on the trip. The train rolls along those tracks through the various stations until they arrive at their final destination.

Many leaders prefer to lead by that method. They value being given a clear direction for the journey. They see their task as one of executing the mission precisely and predictably. This usually assumes that someone else laid the track down for them and established the routines that the conductor will follow. As passengers on a train, we prefer that kind of leader who will get us where we are going reliably on time and on schedule.

If your leadership preferences lean toward the predictable execution of a plan, you want to ensure that your role in the company requires that kind of disciplined ability to follow orders. Does your organization have well-defined tracks laid down for you to lead your team along? If not, you may be in for some challenges. That is one style of leadership, and it is an important one for many organizations.

The second type of leader is the captain of the ship. Think about the time before ships were full of GPS, radar and other electronic gear. Sailing a ship of any kind, even in the early part of the twentieth century, was a big challenge. There were many variables on every voyage that the captain of the ship would encounter.

I am one of those people who really love the *Horatio Hornblower* books and television mini-series. It was a great telling of the tale of what life was like during the 1700s and 1800s with the ships at sea. The first lesson they learned was that the sea is unpredictable. No matter how well you think you know what is going to happen and how well you planned for your journey, what you know for sure is that the unexpected will happen. Huge storms could require you to endure the winds and the rain, hail, sleet, and even snow, depending on where you were sailing. The crew during those times looked to their leader to get them safely through those terrorizing times.

Or a ship might go into a period in which there is a lull and everything just stops. In the doldrums, there is no wind to move you forward. The captain and crew might sit for days and even weeks at a time with a different set of challenges for the leader. The captain has to keep the crew busy and productive, even when there is not much sailing to do.

Then there were all of the variables navigating from place to place, perhaps encountering enemy ships. The whole process of being the captain of the ship in those days was to be able to deal with the unpredictable and make it appear routine.

Ship captains did not have the tracks laid out for them. They may have had a general map of where they were supposed to go and an idea of when they wanted to get there, but it was subject to so many events that could happen along the way. The captains who really made their mark were the people who could dodge and weave with the kinds of changes that were inevitably part of that world.

These type of leaders at sea, as in the *Hornblower* series, took young officers and promoted the best and brightest. You witness all of the experiences and the decisions they had to make along the way at their given rank. They learned from those leaders senior to them to develop their perspective and confidence to face new experiences. Their measure of judgment grew as they had to analyze a situation and to make good choices. Their succession of experience and good decisions led to more promotions. The best mentors modeled leadership, inspired confidence and released the protégé's potential to be great leaders in their own right.

If you are one of those captain-type leaders, you know that you are in for an adventure. At the end of your story, it makes a great tale to tell. But as you are going through it, it can be full of twists and turns, opportunities and disasters, and other things that are very stressful. We always will need people who can handle not only the risk of failure but the possibility of success.

What we are finding in our executive coaching is that we have so many people who thought that their role would be that of a conductor. They expected that their career would follow a predictable progression. Roles like that in companies and organizations still exist. It is more difficult to find them now.

More often than not, people are being thrown into a ship-like leadership challenge. Your employer throws you a captain's hat and says, "Bon voyage!"

So, whether you are looking at your classic pocket watch and saying, "Is the train on time?" or whether you are having people saying, "Aye, aye, Captain!" as they are ready to hoist the sails and shove off, we will help you prepare as a leader in the following chapters – captain, conductor, or otherwise.

EXPLORING THE WILDERNESS

You may be one of those people who had a bad leadership experience. Maybe you were the leader of a team that had the worst season that your team ever had. Perhaps you started a business that did not succeed. You had a dream, and that dream died.

The temptation is to say, "Never again—I do not need the aggravation. I am going to play it safe. I will become one of these people who just float along. At the end of the story, I'll be fine." It is possible that you will be one of those people who can just float along, but life has a way of interrupting us. Those experiences of failure are not things that you should hide and that you should be ashamed to own. In fact, those are the things that help make you stronger. They are part of what makes you who you are.

If you look at any of the great leaders, they all had setbacks. They all had times when things did not go well. Catastrophic decisions led to terrible disasters. The great leaders are the ones who persist. They pick themselves up and try again.

You can look at business leaders, people like Walt Disney, who went bankrupt four times before he finally made a success that others would recognize. What if he quit after the first or second or third time? By the fourth time, you would wonder who could blame him for quitting, but he had the courage of his convictions and his passions. Now we have the benefit of all of the things that he and his creative genius were able to bring.

Many people refer to the example Winston Churchill as a great leader. His early leadership experiences in government combined a quick rise to power and prominence along with some major mistakes. Later he had a period of time that he referred to as his "wilderness years," when he was financially stressed, depressed and discouraged. He was out of favour with the British people, the establishment and the leadership of his country. While he could see things that were going to happen in the future like Britain's vulnerability to a rising Nazi threat, he felt powerless to be able to do anything about it, as his voice was not being heard. Sometimes leadership is not just about the right ideas and perspectives, but also the right time. It is hard to wait for that right time when you are wandering through the wilderness.

Go back to Biblical times. You can think of the great leader Moses. Moses had the best education and the best upbringing in the great empire of Egypt. In spite of that, he ended up for forty years in the wilderness. That is where this phrase originates. During those forty years, he had not been a factor in the history of his people. It was the not until the last forty years that he came back and led his people out of Egypt. That is what people remember of him from the grand story for which he is known.

With people in many different life experiences across the centuries, there is often a "dark night of the soul," as St. John of the Cross described it. You are out of favour and things just are not going well for you. That is when you learn to persist. It gives you a chance to reflect and to truly think about who you are. Through reflection you can learn from your mistakes and identify those things that are most important to you. It becomes an opportunity to come again into a renewed leadership experience. Often those people who have been most successful and have reached the highest heights are the people who are experts in the lowest lows. That combination gives them the sensitivity and a perspective that is very valuable as a leader.

So in your situation, maybe you are just being asked to do a small leadership project. Perhaps you have that experience way back when you said, "I tried that once before. It was a disaster. I am not cut out to be a leader." Give it one more chance. Take what you have learned. Start again with a different perspective on where you are going to go.

Ultimately, you have to choose to lead, as leading is always a choice. It is not enough to say, "I am stuck with a job," or "Somebody forced me into it." If you have the tag of a leader within your group or your business, you are the leader. You have to make the *choice* to lead. It is not enough to sit back and let someone else make those decisions. Someone else may have given you that function or title. At some point along the way, you have to decide to lead and own your future.

WHAT TIME IS IT?

Roger Whitaker used to sing a song entitled "The First Hello, The Last Goodbye." It is a great song for leaders to play regularly. It is not just the dulcet tones of his voice but the message of the lyrics.

It describes how whenever we begin something, there is a sense that we have started the end of it, as well. When we are born, the clock is ticking that will eventually mark our death, too. It is not really a depressing thought, but rather a reminder about our finiteness as human beings. As has been said, time is not a renewable resource.

The good news and the bad news about leadership is that it is always a temporary condition. For those concerned about the challenges to lead, do not worry, it will all be over eventually. For those who thrive as leaders, we too must temper our plans with that same insight.

No matter who you are or what you are being asked to lead, it is always going to be for a limited period of time. You may start an organization and lead it throughout your adult life. You might even retire as the leader of that organization.

All leadership experiences are temporary. You know that there will be a start point and an end point to it. That end point might be a known condition of your leadership role. You may be asked to coach a baseball team for a summer. The summer starts, and then it is done. You might be asked to help with a charitable organization and serve as its executive member for a period of a year. Perhaps you might be someone elected for office for a three-, four- or five-year term.

Your company might ask you to lead a particular project. You are there working with the team for the life of that project. When that project is over, your leadership with that team is over, as well. At some point, your leadership will stop.

If there is one creature that a politician does not want associated with their leadership, it is the duck. That is because the only time commentators make the connection is when the duck is no longer walking or flying with great energy and potential. It is the proverbial lame duck.

Those who are elected to be president of the United States understand that they have a maximum of two terms to serve as leader of the country. Tests of leadership and how the president governs in the first term will be measured against a challenger at the ballot box in four years. A successful incumbent is usually unbeatable. A weak president facing a credible challenger may lose the opportunity to lead again for another term. Decisions are usually made on what priorities to set for the first term with a view to securing an opportunity to have another four years. Then leaders have to adapt to the many unknowns and unforeseen events that often crowd out the best laid plans.

Measurements are taken by the pundits at "the first 100 days" to see what has been organized and accomplished early on in the administration. A year into the term of office, attention begins to turn to the midterm elections, in which seats of all the members of Congress and a third of the Senate are up for election. A compatible Congress helps to enact legislation. An opposition Congress often means gridlock. Once settled, the first year after the midterms creates another window to concentrate on legislation. Then it becomes a return to a presidential race, with so many decisions colored by the effect they might have at election time.

If the president wins reelection, there is a great deal of discussion about how much can be done before their power is sapped by the passage of time.

Often, it is assumed that one good year remains before the cycle of other elections drowns out the leader's voice. That voice begins to take on an accent that sounds peculiarly like a duck. Before most presidents are ready, they cede much of their influence to shape events and their legacy at home. That is when you usually see more overseas visits to try to leave a mark on world affairs. Even there, the fact that their term is ending is included in the calculation of what deals might be made. Everyone soon acknowledges that the president has become the pitiable lame duck.

We lead as stewards entrusted with an opportunity for a period of time. It is not something that is ours. Even though we might contribute great things through our leadership and we might motivate our group to be the most successful that has ever been, still it is only finite. Therefore, we make choices that reflect the fact that it has an end. Knowing this adds humility and urgency to do our best every day with the time we have been given. Tempus fugit!

THE RED MIST

As we have discussed, emotions are an important ingredient of effective leadership. If you want to be a positive influence, you have to know what is going on inside yourself. Just as you can be self-aware about your heart rate being too fast or feeling light-headed, you need to develop the capacity to know your emotional state.

Many leaders make some of their worst mistakes when they are emotionally out of sync. It could be that you are tired and not feeling the energy to make the kind of decision you would normally make. You may feel exhilarated by a great success and want to move on to the next conquest with the same verve. The extreme emotions leave us off balance when it comes to making good choices for ourselves and others. Or you might have seen the Red Mist.

In urban parlance, the Red Mist describes that state where you are overcome with extreme anger or competitiveness that makes it almost impossible to make a good decision. The idea of mist is an apt one. In a misty rain, we think that we can still see, but the mist really does change our perspective. Add to that the color change to red, and you can see how differently our world appears.

Overly optimistic moments can give us a false sense of invincibility. We move forward on the assumption that nothing can get in our way. Our success is inevitable. There is no need to consider all of the risks.

When we are fatigued or depressed, it is easy for us to give up before we begin. We take the previous experience of failure or discouragement and conclude that we are destined to fail again no matter what we choices we might make. Opportunities skip on by us while we are looking down at our feet.

The most dangerous of these is the intense times during the Red Mist. The danger is not just to ourselves but to others since our boiling anger or extreme feelings of competition lead us to attack those in our world to relieve our hostility. The lack of perspective inhibits us from seeing the situation or the perspectives of others accurately. Our anger leads us to assume things about the motives or actions of others that may not be true.

Even if they were true, rarely is striking back the right decision. Caught up in a need for revenge, we stop asking, "What can I do to help?" and now ask, "What I can do to hurt?" That is a very bad place to be. The intensity of our emotional state focuses us on the target, but in that very process of creating greater focus, it narrows our range of vision. We stop seeing alternatives. We just see the bull's-eye.

The same Red Mist applies to us when we see the competition as our target to beat. Winning over the competition is the wrong goal. Our best target is to give our very best every day no matter what the competition is doing. Our standard is improving each day. Like the runner who looks sideways to see where the competition is in the race, leaders slow themselves down if they become emotionally engaged in beating their competition. Learn from your competition? Of course. Adapt to improve your customer service or product quality. There is nothing wrong with being the best. Like so many aspects of life, it is *how* we choose to get there. Being driven by an emotionally charged motivation will increase our chances of making mistakes.

Danger signs often have red to highlight the warnings. The red light. The red stop sign. For *Star Trek* followers – the red alert. When you are too emotionally engaged in the anger or competition of the Red Mist, you will not notice the red warnings of the risks ahead.

Learn to recognize that your emotional intensity may be rising. That is the time to step back and regain perspective. For some leaders, that is a conversation with a member of the team to check your judgment. For others, it is a contact with a mentor to get some sage advice to ensure you have kept the wide point of view to not miss the opportunities or the hazards. Or a good old-fashioned count to ten may be just enough to let the Red Mist clear.

FINDING YOUR CENTER

If you look at the people who have had an enduring influence on others, they are not only in some way central to the lives of others – they have understood themselves. This has made them centered people. It is a strength that helps them achieve what many other people spend their lives wishing they could do.

One of the many sports I enjoyed in school was wrestling. While we were on a wrestling "team," this was very much an individual sport. You were up against an opponent in your weight class, and for each two-minute period you were locked in a battle of strength, skill and endurance. It is one of the most intense sports since everything you are as a person is condensed into every second of those three periods – if you last that long! One of the most critical elements of the sport that you learn early is finding your center of gravity – understanding where that is in your body and how that center can shift as you move. You then need to know where the opponent's center of gravity is and look for ways to move them onto their back for the count. It only takes you losing your balance a few times to appreciate the importance of being centered in that sport.

The same is true of those people who, as people, are centered. It allows them to withstand the challenges and pains of life and to move the obstacles in their way.

A centered person has a clear sense of where they have come from – with all the good and bad that this includes – and where they are going. Not stuck in the past, the centered person is able to correctly assess the present around them. Then they can move forward into a future that they have influenced through their gifts, talents, personality and endurance.

A centered person is not surprised by challenges but accepts them as a positive part of life. They value achievement but understand that success is often connected to failures, with the necessary lessons learned along the way.

In contrast to a self-centered person, a centered person recognizes that they are on this earth to benefit others, not just themselves. It is a mark of maturity and balance that separates them from those who live in the ripples of life, unable or unwilling to make a difference for others.

Becoming a centered person requires reflection. There are some personality types where this comes easily. For others, living in the moment or living in the future means that you do not look back. As with most things in life, a balance is usually healthy. Just as the person who is predisposed to the past needs to value the moment and anticipate the future, there is value in a pause to assess our story to this point.

While everyone cannot do this, people who explore some of their family history through conversations with living relatives or older friends of the family benefit from the experience. Even doing some family tree research can help you see some of the influences that flow into our story. While we are not predestined to replicate our ancestor's careers or personalities, we should not be surprised to see trends also. Sometimes it is not linear from parent to child but traits or predispositions that jump generations or are seen in great-uncles or great-aunts. There is value in knowing our story so learn yours as much as you can. Then be sure to share what you learn with your children or others in your family circle.

Centered people are comfortable in their skin. They have gone beyond self-conscious to be self-aware. This gives them the freedom to confidently be who they are and become who they were meant to be.

The best physicians understand that they are in the business of serving people. The best salespeople are sharing a product or service that they know will improve the lives of others. The best in government really are there to serve the public, not to wield power for their fame or gain. The best in the arts sing, paint, write or use whatever their talent is to inspire, challenge or comfort their audience.

THE SITUATION ROOM

When there is a national or international crisis involving the United States, you will find the president and key diplomatic, military, security and political advisers gathered in a 5,000-square-foot room in the basement of the West Wing of the White House known as "The Situation Room." It was established to link the leaders with sources of real-time information and the communications to respond with decisions that can be carried out. It is there for whatever crisis is facing the country.

One of the things you find out very quickly when you start leading is that there will be a crisis.

"Crisis" is one of those words that is relative. You are unlikely to face the kinds of challenges that a head of government will experience. But if there is something that is testing you or your group with great consequences potentially involved, it is a crisis for you. Rooted in the Greek language but present in many variations of other languages, "crisis" is usually associated with a point of decision or change, with all the risks and rewards that might come from what follows. It is a decision that focuses not just your mind but usually your emotions and often body too as you feel the pressure to deal with the threat or opportunity in front of you.

Some jobs are filled with many crisis moments. Firefighters decide what to do in a fire. Physicians in an emergency room deal with patients who may live or die based on their choices. Police encounter a situation that requires the right response in an instant.

Your leadership may not require you to make those split-second life-or-death decisions in a crisis. But make no mistake about it: You will face decisions that will "sift you" and reveal what you are as a person and as a leader.

Every leader, sooner or later—and usually sooner—will face some kind of crisis.

Crisis management is part of leadership. Given that it usually involves actions or decisions made by others with all the variables of the human race, you can expect the unexpected as you face they key moments in your leadership.

While you cannot predict all the challenges of a crisis, good crisis management involves a number of ways that you can prepare. Training for emergencies is one of the ways first responders prepare to face the decisions they will be required to make. Thinking about their drills is helpful in preparing you, as well.

The firefighters' training involves facing similar challenges that they are likely to face at a fire. The training explores what they can do to stay safe, practice what it feels like to fight a fire, and then undergo the experience to effect a safe rescue or extinguish the fire. Their confidence of knowing what to do in a real fire grows from their successes and failures during their drills. They learn from the manuals and training that build on the experiences of those who have faced similar crises in the past. They benefit from the expertise of scientists who study the characteristics of fire heat, explosions and smoke that occur with different materials and varying conditions. They know their subject area.

Knowledge is vital, but nothing replaces the value of experiencing the act of making the decisions and fighting the fire firsthand. The experience creates an emotional confidence that gives us the power to make decisions.

Our emotions launch our decisions.

That is why you can give two people with different levels of emotion the same set of information, with one making a decision quickly and confidently and the other hesitating with uncertainty. So much of leadership is built upon our previous experiences that have taught us to trust our judgment even if there are unknowns in the equation. A crisis brings out these elements in a leader.

Another crisis management tool is our character. Character is built on our self-image rooted in our upbringing, life experiences and self-confidence. Leaders who are self-aware and who have an honest assessment of who they are as people have a big advantage over a leader who does not know who they really are. Prepare your leadership for the inevitable crises that will come by understanding yourself as a person.

The values that we have understood and owned in our life build the character that we live through day by day. It is never a perfect fit. None of us live up to our ideals every moment of every day. But a person's ideals and values are a good predictor of what to expect from them most of the time. In a crisis, character counts in what our reflex response is likely to be when we do not have the luxury of time to reflect and consider a problem that is not a crisis.

The good news is that facing and responding to a crisis is what it makes for a good story. The bad news is that you will not know how the story will end until it is over. Prepare yourself for a crisis and you will have many more good endings to share.

INVESTING IN YOU

One of the many interesting parts of being a parent is to watch your children save money for a particular purpose. They will do chores that might normally be avoided. They will find extra opportunities to be helpful. If the purchase is especially important to them, they will not spend money on other areas until they have reached their goal. Their investment choices announce their priorities, at least for a little while.

Many leaders make a point in treating every aspect of their job and career as an investment. What they fail to invest in as conscientiously is themselves.

Take care of yourself as a leader. This includes a variety of areas of life, but it certainly includes caring for yourself physically. It is important to get a good night's sleep. In the urgency of being a leader, you might be tempted to concentrate on the latest crisis, feeling like you have to spend every waking moment working on the problem. Instead, make sure you get enough sleep, as your judgment and mood are impacted by the amount of sleep you have each night. Add to that exercise as another way to keep yourself effective as a leader.

In addition to the body, make sure you're taking care of yourself emotionally. Find some things that are going to give you some relief emotionally. For some, that's listening to music. Others are refreshed by reading a book or going to a movie.

Take time to do things that help feed your sense of well-being. Choose to be with people who are nurturing where you can receive as well as give. Be in situations that are going to help you recharge your sense of personal wholeness. Take a walk in the forest. Do whatever it is make sure that those investments in your emotional health are happening.

Challenging times as leaders can draw down to the spiritual aspects of our life more than any other. So if you have a spiritual dimension nurtured in your life, feed that part of your being too. This dimension of your life is often ignored and neglected, especially during the good times, when we do not seem to need it that much. Now is the time to make sure that you are taking advantage of those spiritual resources that are there in your life. For some, it is celebrating their faith. For others, it is the retreat to nature at a cottage or cabin to ponder what is important to you and your life. Engaging our spiritual life reinvigorates our imagination and creativity.

Focus on having a positive social life, as well. Make it a point to get together with interesting people where you can laugh and enjoy being part of a non-business experience where you do not have to be the leader. Having fun with others is a great way to create and store the energy you will need to be around those you will lead back at work.

Do not shortchange the investment in yourself as part of being an effective leader. Great leaders are great people who have a whole-person approach to life. They feed and encourage all of the aspects of who they are as people in order to have something new and fresh to share with those they serve.

SPRINTS AND MARATHONS

A typical career now involves working at many different companies, holding many different positions at the same company, or a combination of the two. Gone are the norms of a generation ago, where one was hired out of college or high school to work at the same firm for the rest of their working life. Even for those who continue with the same government department or corporation, there are many changes in responsibility and even the basic tasks that fill your day. Jobs and careers – it is important to know the difference. Jobs are the sprints, and your career is the marathon of your working life.

It is easy to confuse the two. We become so engaged in the present demands of our job that we often do not step back to discern how this job is a fit or a distraction from our career. This happens to leaders more often than you would imagine. Leaders tend to be the people who step up to the challenge presented and take the next assignment as it comes along. The many sprints blur together until it is difficult to remember that you need to protect your career.

Here are a couple of my many quotes that I use in seminars and coaching.

"You own your career, not your job."

"Be willing to sacrifice any job to protect your career."

Let's unpack those statements.

No matter how great the job is that you're in right now or how successful you have been, your job could disappear in a moment. There are many ways this could happen. You could be fired. You could be promoted. The job might be deemed redundant. It could be outsourced. The company may fold. The government department might make cutbacks.

Always think of any job you are doing as very temporary. Even if it lasts for many years, you need to keep the perspective that your job could be gone tomorrow. That is helpful as a motivator for us to do well with the time we have been given in a job. But just as importantly, it keeps us from becoming so attached to our job that we begin to merge our identity with the job we are doing. People who do not keep their job separate from who they see themselves as are very vulnerable to despair at whatever time their role inevitably ends before or at retirement.

Your career is the marathon in this equation. Technically, some will have multiple careers if you think of people moving between very different roles and industries over their working life. But for our purposes here, we are talking about your employment over a lifetime. The reason that this is an important idea to catch is that many jobs can damage our career. Some jobs may require you to take physical, emotional or even moral risks that can damage your long-term potential. Your job may have you in a toxic work environment where you can become ill. Some work environments are so full of abusive behavior by employers that people feel like they have been poisoned emotionally. In rare cases, you may be asked to do something that you believe is unethical or immoral. If your job is the only consideration, you may choose to stick it out. But if you recognize that your long-term career is what must be protected and preserved, you may find that it is wise to quit the job you are in rather than compromise your future.

The same is true with our family life. Do not let a job rob you of what you believe is most important when it comes to investing time into the lives of your spouse and children. Many people have learned the hard way that after the gold watch (rare now) is given by the company, you fade into the distant memory of the organization very quickly. If your job has caused you to fade into memory with your family, you will have a difficult time rekindling those relationships.

There are some times in life when we do not have the choice of a great job. Working is usually better than not working when you need to pay the bills. Being out of work has significant emotional and self-image costs to be considered, as well. However, if you are in a job that is not the right fit for you, be sure that you are aggressively doing what needs to be done to get a better one. That might mean more education or skills as well as hunting for that other opportunity.

You may have a career plan that sees your present assignment as a temporary one. It is tempting to portray your current job as much less than you could handle. It is just a stepping stone on the path to bigger and better things. While there is nothing wrong with planning your career (do!) and having ambition (good in itself), there are risks for you. Those who are your leaders might believe that you are not giving your best to your present role. Team members may suspect that you are not really committed to them since you see them as a temporary stopping point. The balancing principle is to be a good steward of the assignment you currently have by always giving your best. Opportunities have a way of finding those who keep their eye on the ball more than those who are too often trying a gambit to make their next conquest.

It is not a bad thing to have some emergency money saved up to give yourself the flexibility to walk away from the wrong job in order to protect your career. Treasure and invest in career decisions that will give you a lifetime of satisfaction when you retire.

THE REAL DEAL

One of the first places I first studied leadership was in a high school course with my wonderful history teacher, Jerry Dimmick. This was back in the good old days of high school, when they had a lot of flexibility in the what was taught. He created the curriculum that we studied for that course.

In order to better understand leadership, we studied some of the great leaders from history. We explored the history of people like Churchill, Lenin, the presidents Roosevelt, Stalin, Mao Tse-tung, and many others from different ages and places.

Some of these leaders served their people well, while others had a terrible impact on humanity. The process led us to begin thinking about the nature of leadership and what goes into making a leader successful and effective. What was that "extra something" in the leader that makes him or her great compared to their contemporaries and their peers? What a great introduction into a topic that would be helpful throughout life, whether we happened to be leaders or followers at any given moment.

One of the things that you learn very quickly is that leadership is a lifelong learning event. It is not something that you ever truly perfect, since the circumstances of the world around you are constantly changing. You may finish with a particular role of leadership, but there is always something more to learn, and that is what makes it an exciting and dynamic experience.

Churchill was one of the greatest leaders of the twentieth century, but he was always "Winston Churchill" first and foremost. He was the same Winston Churchill serving as a young army officer in far-flung places of the British Empire. He would later adventure as a war correspondent following in the footsteps of the great war correspondents of that age, like the legendary Charles Williams.

Later, Churchill was a young cabinet member in the British government before WWI, in which he served as the Lord of the Admiralty. He was the same man during his wilderness years of the 1930s, when he was out of power and out of favor as the world was creeping toward WWII.

Winston was that right person to defend the United Kingdom when the Second World War finally came, as he had correctly foreseen. He led Britain to endure against all odds. Ultimately, the effort of the United Kingdom and the Commonwealth countries was just enough to hang on until they were joined by the Americans under President Franklin D. Roosevelt after the attack on Pearl Harbor.

Finally, he was dismissed from office in the next election by a war-weary public.

Throughout all of this, Winston Churchill was still Winston Churchill. He was certainly seasoned with the experiences he had, but he was essentially who he was throughout his life experience.

The same is true with most great leaders. They have a good sense of who they are, and they use that authentically.

What are the things that are going into your life experience that can help you be an effective leader? Think of the things that make you special. Every one of us has a unique combination of experiences, the choices we made and the roads not travelled. Together, they make us who we are.

You have reached a certain age going through experiences at school, sports, groups and work. You have a certain set of parents. You have a certain family background. It may have been an easy one, or it may have been a tough one. You may have had the experience of having money in your family, or maybe it was tough for your family to make ends meet.

All of these things mold and shape us into who we are. The universities you attended or did not attend all take us down a path. They combine into the story that makes you who you are today, and your leadership will flow through that experience.

Recognize that as you look at great leaders, you are not them. You will be your own brand of leader. The temptation is to try and mimic them. I cannot be Winston Churchill, and neither can you. You cannot be Martin Luther King, John F. Kennedy, Franklin D. Roosevelt, Margaret Thatcher or Teddy Roosevelt. For the Canadians, we can include Pierre Trudeau.

Any great leader who had a great impact on their world lived a different tale than your story. Learn from their experiences and the ways that they handled challenges and crises. There are lessons from all the leaders who succeeded and those who failed. But remember, you cannot be them; you need to be *you*.

How can you be *you*? How did we let Reagan be Reagan? It begins at the same place. We have to give ourselves permission to be authentic. That is not our lazy self or "I could care less" self, but our best self. If we took the best of who we are, we have something to offer those we will lead.

THE RETURN OF THE KING

In my favorite work of fiction, *The Lord of The Rings* by J. R. R. Tolkien, the character Aragorn was faced with questions about his past and his future. He was descended from a long line of kings, but at that time, no king sat upon the throne in his kingdom of Gondor.

Aragorn was torn between a duty to lead and the haunting fears that he would make the same mistakes that his ancestors did. Through the encouragement of Arwen, his fiancée, and others, Aragorn finally entered the battle as king and eventually sat upon that throne.

In his struggle, Aragorn's tale reminds us of many of the same struggles we all have when we try to explore who we are and where we might fit into the larger world around us.

Like Aragorn, we all begin with a past. At the moment we are born, we have history. Some of that is well-known to us early on. For others of us, it might be something much less clear. But we are all born with certain unchangeable pieces of the puzzle.

We are born at a point in time. We are a child of the _____ (fill in the blank). If you were a child of the '60s, you will have a different outlook from someone who is born in the '70s or '80s. Those who grew up during the great depression of the 1930s were very affected by those years. They tended to worry more about money and were very frugal, having seen how long and deep hard times might be. If you were of the generation from World War II, you are of a generation who had to face the horrors of Nazi Germany. Whenever you are born, it makes your story a different one from those who began life in different times. It is part of who you are.

Where you were born matters, too. If you were born in even the poorest areas of the United States or Canada, you have many significant advantages over much of the rest of the world. If you were born in a poorer country, you have some additional challenges.

A person's IQ is a measure of their "intelligence quotient," but it does not how well you will apply your intelligence. So being born with advantages or disadvantages does not decide your fate. Many people do not take advantage of the opportunities of their country to get an education and develop a worthwhile career.

Others will use their disadvantages as a motivation to overcome and succeed in spite of their challenges. That becomes part of their story.

There are many other parts of our beginning that were not our choice. We did not choose our parents, the first communities where we lived, what schools we attended or our socioeconomic status. The color of our skin, our first language and so many other traits are set by nature and the choices of others while we are young.

As time passes, we begin to have choices that start to define us differently even from our parents and siblings. But it is not until later in life that some of the most significant choices can be made by us.

Far into our later years in life, we will continue to be followed by some of the unchangeable elements of our history.

For Aragorn, he could not escape and ultimately was most fulfilled in taking up the sword and crown that were both his past and his destiny.

What are some of the facts of your life? How have they impacted who you are and how you see yourself? What is unchangeable in the story of you? How might that influence your destiny as a leader?

Great leaders have appeared in the most unlikely times and from some of the most unlikely places.

You might be one of them.

THE HEART OF THE LEADER

As important as it is in a leadership position to use your head, it is not enough. As leaders, the challenge is to not only use our heads but to use our hearts, as well. The great leaders are people who can combine both head and heart. They can understand the facts—the ideas that are true, the tasks that need to be done and all of the elements that go into decision making. However, they never lose sight of the people.

They recognize the impact that their decisions are having on the people that are in their zone of influence through their leadership. That does not mean that they always get to change their answers. In war, great leaders had to make decisions that often sent young men and women into harm's way, and sometimes to their death. People who assign rescue teams often know that the people going in to do the rescue are at risk, and occasionally they sadly sacrifice their lives to save others. Sometimes leadership requires those hard choices. The people who make those kinds of decisions, if they are great leaders, are always aware of the human cost side of the equation. They not only know the consequences of their decisions – they feel the impact on the individuals in their team. When a leader puts herself or himself in the place of those on their team, they can begin to not only know but also feel what their team is going through. That's a leader who understands. That kind of leader will made wise decisions because they count the cost.

Great leaders are not measured only by whether or not they are right. It is not enough just to be right. That is a good starting point and a good place to be; you want to be right, but that is not enough. If you are going to be effective as a leader, you have to go beyond that. Leaders are able not only be right, but to do things in the right way, at the right time, with the right motives and with the right attitude. That comes to a fundamental understanding of the nature of effective leadership.

The great leaders, the ones who had the most positive influence down through history, are the people who had a common characteristic. They had a mentor's heart.

When I say, "mentor," this does not mean that they are walked all over or are told what to do by others. Instead, whatever they are doing comes from them having a desire to have others succeed. They put the well-being of their team members, customers, and other stakeholders above their own self-interest. They choose to lead in order to make a difference for the benefit and development of others. Their motivation is not to accumulate more power and authority.

In the British tradition of the government, the equivalent of the United States cabinet secretary is called a "minister." The first among the ministers is the Prime Minister of Great Britain, or Canada, or Australia, or other places that use that model. This is a helpful reminder because as ministers, they are to minister to others. They are there to serve other people through their leadership. They are there to benefit others.

Someone who comes to leadership with a minister's heart asks, "How can I make you successful? What can I do to make you successful in the job or in the opportunity that you have? How can I serve my clients better? How can I serve the public better? How can I make a difference that will benefit other people?"

If that becomes part of your leadership style and the heart part of your leadership, then your head is going to make much better decisions.

One of the risks of leadership is having and using power. As was said so long ago, power corrupts and absolute power corrupts absolutely. As leaders, one of the antidotes for that is to say, "I am not here for me. I am not about getting my power and glory so it all works out for my benefit. I am here to serve other people. I am here to make a difference in the lives of these other people."

Developmental leadership is a concept that says that I am here to serve, not here to be served.

Serving others does not bring a lack of respect. This is one of those paradoxes in life. We would assume that if we become concerned about other's success, then we are not going to be a success. The reality is quite the opposite, however. People who spend their lives investing in other people trying to make them successful are the ones who become more successful themselves in the long run. They usually are much more content with the life they have lived when they look back at their story. These leaders earn a positive legacy with the people they served.

We have all met those leaders who have the tyrannical attitude that others are there to serve them. Before long, they become very lonely and ineffective. It does not take long for people start to work against them to undermine their authority and leadership. A commitment to serving others will liberate not only yourself but also the people around you to be effective.

DECISIONS

Being a leader is about making decisions. Leading with your head means that you have to make choices. One of the tough parts of leadership is that you as a leader will make decisions. Those decisions need to be informed by reliable information. You do make better decisions when you have reliable information. When you can look at the different things that go into the decision-making process, you have confidence.

As a leader, you need to do your homework. You will want to make sure that you have people around you who are going to thoughtfully share their facts, ideas, and perspectives. Then, when you are going to make a decision, you have the benefit of the best information as well as the decision-making process. If you want to make wise decisions, you look not only at the past perspective of where we have been and the present perspective of where we are today, but you also need to make decisions that make sense for the future. That is because you have to lead not only for today but for tomorrow as well. Make decisions that are going to be helpful for your organization, your company, or your government down the road, as well as for the present time. That challenge is very difficult for leaders in an age of short-term measurements and quarterly results.

Leaders try to balance pressures from one side that says, "We want to stay like we were; we want to hold on to the past. We want to continue the legacy that we have as an organization." The past can be very important.

You also may have pressures just for today: "We have to solve the problems of today. We have to just get through today – that is enough. We do not have time to think about tomorrow. We do not have time to worry about the past. This crisis is now."

Then you have other situations with pressure about the next five or more years. Five years can seem like an eternity when you look at business planning. It seems like the future is way out there in the mist. Yet to be responsible as the leader of an organization, you have to consider those longer-range plans, too.

Leadership is very much a process of balancing these competing interests and making wise decisions. If there is one thing that defines the great leaders, it is that they were wise people. Wisdom is more than just knowledge. Wisdom is the ability to take the knowledge and apply it in the most effective way for the circumstances that you face. Wise leaders are able to take what is true, what is good and what is possible. They then dream a little bit beyond that so that the organization or the people who are involved can go beyond themselves. It becomes a comfortable stretch.

Wisdom and balance are necessary, but there has to be decision making. As a leader who cares, you want to make good decisions. You have to use the best resources that you have. As with any process, you try to take it bit by bit and try to make sense of the decisions that you have to make. Break them down into smaller decisions. Break them down into ways of thinking about particular problems, and then expand it and say, "If we do this, how does it affect the opportunities over here?"

Just as we have blind spots to remember as drivers, leaders typically have blind spots when it comes to leadership as well. Many executives may have a blind spot about themselves that hinders them from seeing how their behavior or decisions impact those with whom they serve. Mentors, coaches and good friends can help them become aware of those weak areas and then remind them to check that spot again before making a move. Other leaders have a blind spot when it comes to a particular team member where they do not recognize a problem because they enjoy them as a person. It can affect their judgment. Executives often have a piece of their responsibilities where they regularly do not see the opportunities or challenges clearly. That can be a function of a lack of experience. It might be an area of the business that the executive does not relate to easily. Knowing this weakness will minimize mistakes.

This is why you should remember decisions you made in the past. It takes confidence to make decisions. The more decisions you have successfully made in your life, the more confident you will be of new decisions you face. That is why we encourage community organizations and schools to give the young people in their world opportunities to be leaders sooner rather than later. Do not wait until they are 25, 30 or 50 before you say, "Now it is time for you to be a leader."

Give them opportunities to lead within their organization as class leaders, school leaders, leaders in sports, or leaders in community groups. Do not wait until they are mature and out there in the great wide world before they have an opportunity to taste a leadership experience. All of these decisions and group dynamics involved in leadership are very valuable. As with all experiences in life, it is great for you to have them early so that you get a sense of not just the facts of being a leader but what it feels like to lead.

I DOUBT IT!

To lead is to doubt. All leaders need permission to have doubts. If you are worried that great leaders only have great certainty, you can breathe out now. Relax. It is okay to be a leader who doubts. In fact, doubt is probably one of the healthiest signs that you can have. Having said that, doubt is not the reason to stay away from making decisions.

To lead is to decide.

Doubt is actually a healthy experience, as it reminds us of our finiteness. None of us can see everything or know everything that is going on. So we have valid reasons to doubt. Whenever we make decisions, we always make it with the humility that comes from being truly human.

It is helpful to learn the difference between certainty and confidence. There are very few times that a leader has absolute certainty that a decision is not only the very best one but that it will all work out as planned. Yet many leaders wait to make a decision until they have certainty. As Donald Rumsfeld said so famously, "There are known knowns. These are things we know that we know. There are known unknowns. That is to say, there are things that we know we don't know. But there are also unknown unknowns. There are things we don't know we don't know."

It is worthwhile to reread that a couple of times because it is so true. Leaders must be able to discern whether what they are considering is in fact something that is known or unknown, along with the possibility that we do not know that we do not know!

Statements like that and others point us away from an arrogant view of certainty. The preferred approach is not certainty but confidence.

If certainty is 100%, then confidence is everything below that mark. Confidence is a sliding scale that allows us to assess whether our decision is based on a great deal of evidence that is clear, as in 80% or 90%. Perhaps the evidence is mixed and it requires a judgment call where our confidence is only 50%. Some decisions actually fall below that, when you might have multiple options and the best option might only be 40% but the others have even less confidence.

The lower our confidence, the more we will need to create alternatives or contingency plans in case our best choice fails. What many leaders miss is that even a 99% scenario deserves a backup plan because there still remains that slight possibility that all will not work out as we thought.

When sharing our decisions, it is helpful that others understand that we are "assuring" and not "guaranteeing" a particular result. We make our decisions confidently (there's the word!) and pass that confidence along to others. As a helpful role model, we do not want to give those serving with us the false impression that they will have more than confidence in their experiences, as certainty is not really an option.

Decisions, of course, often are not just a matter of what choice to make but when to make it. Many great decisions were disasters because of when they were made. Timing matters.

It is helpful to learn and teach the phrase "good enough to go" to ensure that projects finish. Combinations of emotions like fear and uncertainty can keep a project in beta stage when it should have long since gone to market. As long as it is still in development, we can believe that there is no risk of failure. Once a product is released, we then have to live with the evaluations as to its success or lack thereof. Keeping a product longer than you should is also a failure since you cannot earn or benefit from its release as intended.

The other hindrance can be personality types that lean toward the perfectionist. Very few things could not be reexamined, reviewed or revised one more time. Some reviews are useful. Many revisions can improve the product. You do want to produce reliable products that are excellent and valued for the care that went into their design. Perfectionists will, by nature, want to take one more look at it. Leaders recognize when something has passed the threshold of "good enough to go" so that the product can be available. It is a sad truth but few people or things achieve anything close to perfection, so the quest for the perfect anything is a fool's errand. Instead, the test is whether it exceeds expectations, serves the consumer well and does the company proud. That's enough, and get on with it. Perfectionists are best found doing hobbies where they can take all the time they want to take as no one is depending on it. Business must keep going.

As you approach a decision, ask how urgently the decision needs to be made *for best results*. Many leaders prefer to defer a decision if it is not really required. That postpones any risk of failure. Sometimes decisions should be left until later. But that only applies if we include the "for best results" clause in the process. Making early decisions sometimes will help us to avoid much larger and more costly decisions later even though technically they were not required to be made.

That should make it easier for us to learn from our mistakes. If you only have certainty and something does not turn out for the best, you will begin to undermine your confidence in everything you think you know as a leader. However, with a humble spirit, you will be able to expect the best from your best decisions but face challenges honestly when things do not go as planned. Having doubt does not mean that the decision you are going to make is a bad one; it just means you have some doubt.

Part of the experience of being a leader is to learn both to doubt and then how to resolve that doubt as much as you can. Maybe it is by obtaining more information, or perhaps it through checking with more people who can give you advice. This is where your key staff and, in some cases, your mentor or coach can help you sort through the issues involved in the decision to be made.

Do not discount the importance of front-line personnel as well as those more senior in the organization. Often, those closest to the place where the decision will have the greatest impact will have helpful perspectives. They may know details that could change your decision if considered. Remember, being an executive is about executing the decisions. It does not mean that you already know everything there is to know.

Whatever the choice may be, going through a healthy decision-making process will help you gain confidence in the decision you need to make. Make the decisions with your heart and your head, and you will make them much more successfully.

CREATING YOUR BIOGRAPHY

Every day, we are adding to our biography. Some days might be a very short entry. Other days could be one of our turning points of personal history where we begin a new chapter. Often, we are surprised by those most important days since when the day began, it seemed like just another day. Even as we experience those big days, we might not realize how important they are until later. A decision made, a person we met, or an opportunity we chose could turn out to be very significant to our story. Who knew?

If you were outlining your autobiography, what would you include? This is different from our resume, where we record the past jobs we held. How do the unseen forces in your life impact the collection of jobs that we call a career?

It can be helpful to come up with a shorter version that might fit a Wikipedia entry that includes the big events. Perhaps you could tell your tale as a short story. Remember the questions your elementary school teacher would ask in constructing a story? Who would be the main characters? What were the crossroads? What was the setting? What was the challenge, conflict or crisis? How did it turn out?

There are some planned additions to our biography. How much we invest in time and energy into our high school life may affect our range of choices for university. Whether we decide to go to college or not can change the trajectory of our life. What college or university we chose will influence the rest of our story, not just through our studies but also through the relationships we develop with the professors and students we meet.

We choose to marry or not and who that will be. Having or not having children will change us. What jobs we take along our career path – these factors all become part of our continuing adventure.

Some of those choices will enrich our lives, while others may haunt us if we are not careful. They are all part of our biography.

As you speak with people at the end of their career, most are surprised where they ended up. Many exceeded their best hopes for a future. Others ended up doing something that was completely different from what they planned when they were leaving university. Some find that their meaning and purpose have changed over the decades as they have matured.

What are some of the big-ticket decisions that you have made in your biography? As you look back at them, did they seem as big then? How have they turned out compared to your hopes and dreams? What or who made them successful?

Who are the people in your life who were there for you? How did they encourage your success? What did it cost them to be part of your story? How do you believe that they feel it was beneficial for them?

Who are some of the heroes in your biography? Was it a special teacher who introduced you to a key subject or who believed in your potential when no one else did? Did you have someone who mentored you? Was there someone who was there for you during a dark time of your life? What did they do or say that made you feel good about who you are?

Have you ever taken the time to give them some feedback on how they were part of your life story? Have you ever thanked them? They are certainly a part of you.

Your story will continue to evolve as you journey through your life and career. Like all stories, it only represents a point of view. But knowing your story will help you give your working life a context. For many people, the exercise of thinking about their story becomes an adventure of discovery.

People who understand and own their story with all the good and the bad (and sometimes we have to add the ugly too!) are usually more effective in what they do because they know who they are.

ORANGES AND BANANAS

David Garshowitz is a longtime pharmacist at York Downs Pharmacy in Toronto. He is a sage who likes to reflect not only on his professional life but also on life itself. David produced a YouTube video called *The Seven Vitalities* that presented a way of looking at life that leads to a healthier worldview even as you take care of yourself and others. Following *The Seven Vitalities* is a strategy toward a healthier lifestyle for longevity and wellness.

In that presentation, David includes congeniality as one of the vitalities. He discusses how long-term and relational stresses can be the trigger that leads to a compromised immune system. Once our immunity is reduced, it is easier for us to be vulnerable to disease, inflammation and many other health risks. So many of these stresses can be resolved by a commitment to congeniality.

Congeniality, like love, has more to do with our will than our emotions. Just as we make decisions and commitments to love someone, we can also choose to be congenial. By temperament or by practice, many people seem to have an easier time being congenial than others do. You can probably easily think of someone who is a congenial person. They are easy to get along with, make you feel comfortable and seem to know how to make their relationships work.

Look below the surface of this temperament and you will find some choices that created the commitment to be a congenial person. From there, the skills were developed to practice congeniality until like any skill, it becomes second nature. Just as nations make treaties to define their relationships with other countries, we decide how we will value or ignore others in our lives. One of the reasons that we practice social skills is to help us function more effectively in a community. We practice manners for addressing others or eating together because it makes the experience more positive and pleasant.

Many leaders underestimate the importance of being congenial. With a sharp focus on the bottom line and productivity, it is easy to ignore some of the process questions that keep the relationships strong between those who must pull together to reach the goals of the organization. Social cues help us reduce the friction of individuality that can lead to people only serving their own interests rather than the benefit of others. The congenial leader will achieve better long-term results from his or her team because of the respect that it demonstrates. It also becomes an example to follow that sets a tone for the other working relationships within the organization too.

Being congenial is not just about relationships but how we look at our leadership as well. Some leaders panic or get angry when all is not going their way. Whether it is fear or anger, both will unbalance the canoe. Leaders who have developed congeniality have a more balanced approach to both successes and setbacks.

One of the phrases David Garshowitz would use is "What you lose in the bananas you make up in the oranges." It is a philosophy that steps back from the moment to have a positive perspective that things will work out if you stay calm. When a setback comes, deal with it but do not fear it. Life and business have a way of balancing out if you give it a chance. Similarly, do not become overly enthused about your successes because they too will ultimately be balanced along the way.

Choosing to be congenial means that you will look for ways to make relationships work well. Leaders understand that energy is gained or lost in how well relationships are working. We benefit from having the same commitment to being congenial as we do to being accurate or thorough. It is a similar test of our persistence.

As David points out, congeniality is not only good for business—it can also be good for your health.

Enjoy the bananas and the oranges as they come along.

PEN OR PENCIL

Some people love pencils. In some professions, they are very helpful as you can sketch or doodle with the confidence that the other end of the pencil is there to erase anything you wish to change. I remember what a big deal it was in school to get permission from your teacher to graduate from a pencil to a pen.

It was a "write" of passage for those of us who wanted to express ideas as well as a rite of passage in our early academic life. The complication of a pen, of course, is that it is much more difficult to erase what you wrote. Efforts to do so usually made the area smudge and if you were not careful, you had a hole in your paper. Eventually you understood why they taught us to take a ruler and strike out the incorrect or unwanted words with a straight line through them. Interestingly, it was not a blotting out of the words or an attempt to "x" it out. Your ill-conceived or alternative word selection was there for anyone to see. It seemed like such a relief to get to the stage of typewriters with "corrector ribbons" and eventually correction fluid. Once you could use a word processor, the errant words could just "poof" into cyberspace, as if they never happened. While great for changes, it was most unfortunate when unintentionally erased without backup – but that is another story…

Leaders face the pen-pencil dilemma regularly. In part, it becomes a style of leadership. Will you be the kind of leader who will only write in pencil with your eraser handy? Or are you the kind of leader who uses pen, crosses out mistakes for all to see, and then moves forward?

As many leaders have learned the hard way (and many more have never seemingly learned), when you lead, you will make mistakes. Some might have been your best effort but were not correct. Others might reflect poor judgment. Whenever a mistake is recognized, the question becomes: "What do you do next?"

Many leaders opt for the pencil and eraser. They will try to erase any evidence of a mistake once it happens. It is not enough to put your best foot forward; it has to be a perfect foot, always placed exactly right every time. Making mistakes or even misjudgments is so feared that we will do anything we can to cover up the errors. The effect is that we are predisposed to cover-up. That usually does not end well and often becomes a larger problem than the original error.

Taking the "pen" approach to leadership takes a stronger self-image that has a humble perspective about our ability to be perfect. We are not. We have not been. We will not be. AND THAT'S OKAY!

The good news is that leaders do not have to be perfect. Scoring your leadership is like being a hitter in baseball. If you are going to be a great hitter in baseball, hitting .300 consistently is an achievement. But what does that mean? It means that you swing at pitches and you hit around three times out of ten. The converse is also true: Someone with a great batting average may have missed hitting half of the time or more.

The same concept is true with leadership. We must think of ourselves in that batting context vs. being perfect every time. The perfection trap is something that will make you ineffective in everything that you do because you will always be worrying about making a mistake. Let me say it again: You do not need to be perfect! You just need to be doing the best job you can for the right reasons and with the right attitude. You will make mistakes and when that happens, own it and move on.

Leaders learn to enjoy the flavor of crow. If you have not "tasted crow," then you probably have not led for very long. As they say, you have to eat crow as part of the leadership experience when you fail. The taste of crow is healthy. It reminds us that we are only human and that any leadership depends on other people. As leaders, while we may be the ones making a decision, as former President Harry Truman said, "The buck stops here." The same thing applies with the crow, as the crow often stops there, too. So, a little taste of crow gives us some humility, a useful ingredient in effective leadership.

Do not be afraid to put away that pencil with its eraser and opt for a pen. Those who follow you will learn the value of transparency. When you make mistakes, you will avoid the tendency to cover up the fact that you are only human too.

ARTS AND SCIENCES

Leadership is more art than science. There is an art to leading people successfully. Elements that go into leading others are not easy to follow like a recipe. Leadership is more complex and nuanced.

How did you learn how to lead? In addition to formal academic or employment positions, we often find hints of the leaders we will become from our childhood experiences where we were able to shine either in sports, a skill or a talent. These were the moments when there was something we were able to do that stood out in front of an audience or group. You accepted and succeeded at meeting the responsibility to perform with all the stress that those moments held. How we make those choices and how we deal with those experiences down through our lifetime is part of the shaping and formation of who we become as adults.

The question continues as to whether our leaders are born or made. As is true of all long-standing debates, the answer is probably both. It might be more accurate to say that we are born into leadership in the sense that the combination of genes and upbringing can combine to give us some of the tools that make leaders effective. However, that is not universally true. Many children of leaders choose to go in the opposite direction. That could be from the type of leadership their parent(s) used. Sometimes they saw firsthand the painful experiences that some leaders must endure and chose to never go there. But it is never a surprise when daughters or sons of a leader emerge as leaders themselves.

Undoubtedly there are some people who are gifted as leaders, and they have a special potential as leaders. Former Canadian leadership candidate and Federal Finance Minister Donald McDonald once referred to leaders needing the "royal jelly." It was a queen bee reference of having something that can influence others to work with you effectively. There is a charisma factor in many leaders.

There is also an experience and trust element. All of these are exercised as part of the art of leadership. People who are gifted as leaders earn that trust on a faster track than most do. Sometimes it is through their resume and through the experiences they have had and the confidence that they have. Often it is through the authenticity of who they are. If they are gifted as leaders, they will have a special potential to do that which can give them a real edge.

Just as there are late bloomers in physical development, there are late bloomers in leadership, too. Some people suddenly appear to be ready to lead although they may have had little experience before. This could be due to the combination of emotional and social factors that suddenly mesh. Or it may be that there have not been opportunities to lead before where their abilities could have been recognized. Sometimes, a person just was not ready to jump into the water.

You may look at your life – you may be called upon to lead a team or to help out with an organization or whatever – and you look at it and say, "I can do this. I will learn from it and I will make mistakes, but I can do this."

Perhaps you have leadership in your DNA. Maybe you have that natural charisma that makes others want to follow you. You may just be the person who was tapped on the shoulder as the most likely not to say no. How you became leader is less important once you have the role. Natural leaders can forget that their purpose is to serve others. Family dynasties can produce a sense of entitlement.

Only those who serve others well are likely to continue to have the trust needed to lead effectively. Executives who have a good sense of who they are and what will serve the greater good of their stakeholders are worthy of the title of leader.

However you became leader, choose to serve others well.

LQ = IQ + EQ + SQ

Many leadership courses concentrate on knowledge and expertise as the way to become an effective leader. Know more than anyone else, and they will follow you. As an executive coach, I can tell you that knowledge is powerful and useful. What I can also tell you is that a stellar command of the facts is not enough.

Lead with your head, your heart and your hope.

All three are very important to effective leadership, whether you are leading a small group or a team or a country. All of the three elements of leadership need to be functioning well in any leader.

Put another way for our more mathematical friends, the formula is LQ = IQ + EQ + SQ. Or for the rest of us, to have your best leadership quotient, you need to combine your intelligence quotient with your emotional quotient and your social quotient.

When IQ was first added to the popular consciousness, educators and scientists were careful to stress the importance of the notion of a "quotient." That spoke to a person's potential but did not serve as a guarantee. Only the IQ that was put to work could reach its potential. A person with a high IQ but who did not study might be surpassed on a test by someone with a lower IQ but who worked hard at their studies.

Over time, we have come to realize that learning is so much more than just IQ. Even what we call IQ may be subject to social and cultural bias depending on how it is measured.

For our purposes here, we are including the concepts of our intuition and abilities in our intellect, emotional and social skills. The most effective leaders can draw on all these elements of who we are and use them effectively.

Leaders who do not know their subject will lose respect. No one wants to follow someone who does not know what she or he is doing or where they are going. Not knowing the content of your responsibilities means that you are not concerned with a successful outcome. Most people do not want to associate with that type of leader for long.

If an executive does not know how to relate to the emotional side of his team, they may agree with her or him but will not care. People get frustrated. Team members celebrate. Tragedy can interrupt someone's life. Leaders who are closed or inept in their emotional life will fall short. Emotional connections are based on reciprocity. People open up about how they are feeling and find acceptance, rejection or indifference. Where they find acceptance, they will be more likely to trust and support the leader.

Where a leader lacks social skills and intuition, the team will sense this and respond awkwardly. What could have been a positive moment of working together becomes a hunt by each of the participants for a means of escape. People are drawn to positive social experiences and avoid those that have a history of not ending well.

Most people do not start out with a well-balanced leadership quotient. Use your strengths and work on your weak areas. If you are not the smartest person in the room, make sure you are the best prepared. If you do not relate well emotionally, practice the gestures that society uses to express emotions like a sympathy note, a congratulations email or some other recognition. If you struggle socially, make sure you have a socially adept person coordinating and carrying those occasions that are not comfortable for you. Showing your support socially and being with the team on those occasions will go a long way.

Of course, if you can add experience and charisma, then... well, that is another formula.

THE LIGHTHOUSE AND THE LEADER

As you travel around different countries and see the beautiful architecture that goes into the variety of shapes and sizes that are there, the one common characteristic of the lighthouses is that they are built to last. Otherwise, they would have been gone a long time ago.

A lighthouse is a great image for leadership. If you are a leader in a corporation, government, or nonprofit organization, the expectations are high, the opportunities are great, and the responsibilities are even greater.

How do you picture leadership? What images do you think of when you think of a leader? Sometimes it is individuals. They can be great leaders from history or other leaders whom they have read about in biographies or even in movie roles they portrayed. Seeing faces when you think of leadership is helpful. However, we also want to use some other symbols that can be powerful reminders of what effective leaders are all about.

The lighthouse is one of those symbols of an effective leader. Take a moment to think about it. How does a lighthouse remind you of leadership? Here are some ideas to add to your list.

Lighthouses are built to last. They must weather the storms that will come. Leaders need to be durable, too. No matter how great a particular day, week, month or year is going, you understand as a leader that it is only a matter of time before you will face some trials and tribulations—the storms of leadership. You have to be well prepared for that. A sturdy leader has a clear understanding of self, a sense of mission and a willingness to endure. These are qualities for the leader who is committed to the success of their team.

With lighthouses we see many different types: the shapes and sizes are variable, the heights are different, and the positioning changes along the shoreline. There are many aspects that go into the choices in the design of a lighthouse. It is not just a matter of the exterior paint colors or the historical period when that model was used. The mission of that lighthouse was included in the design decisions.

Was it primarily a navigation beacon, or was it warning of a dangerous reef or shoal? Was it tall to see over the cliffs nearby, or was it low with a focus on the near shore? The right lighthouse for the location and time is essential.

This is true for leaders, as well. There are many different types of leaders. If you think of the great leaders in history, you can come up with a variety of names of very effective leaders in different places and at different times. They all had some common characteristics as effective leaders, but there were many differences, too. The times in which they lived and the challenges they faced shaped them and the people they led. Just as with the variety of lighthouses, effective leaders do not all look the same.

Great leaders do not come from a cookie cutter. Their leadership reflects who they are as people. They are authentic.

One of the roles we have as an executive coach is to assist leaders to step back and understand who they really are. What are your strengths, talents, abilities and gifts that you have been given? What are the education and other resources you bring to the job? Then, we work together on the question of how "you can be you" as an effective leader.

Another feature of a lighthouse is that it provides a point of reference. Someone who is sailing can spot the lighthouse, and it assists in coordinating where they are on a map. This acts like a beacon to mariners to know better where they are. This then is used in navigation to continue on their course in order to arrive at their destination.

Leaders are a point of reference for those in their organization. Team members look to the leader as a beacon to not only guide them for the future but to tell them in the moment where they are and how they are doing. This can be a heavy responsibility for leaders as you are aware that you are a work in progress, too. You have your strengths and weaknesses. It can be uncomfortable to have people measuring their progress in relation to the cues they receive from you, the leader. It can be very daunting at times, but in fact that is an important part of being a leader.

If you are part of an educational institution, the period when a certain president was in charge often defines much of the era at the school. It is not only the changes in the buildings built or the evolution of the academic programs of the school that are remembered. Presidents or principals often set the tone for their school that is felt and remembered. The nature of the president's leadership marks the institution.

Lighthouses and leaders share another characteristic. The light of the lighthouse goes around in all directions. It does not just concentrate straight ahead. Most lighthouses spin completely and cover the 360 degrees of their area. This strengthens the value of the lighthouse as it reaches the various vantage points in its area. Some observers will be closer, while others are further away.

As the light spins, it can be seen by people far and wide. It is a source of information and point of reference for all of those people, and that is true for leaders, as well. Leaders have to be able to look in all directions. Sometimes there is a myopia that can occur with leaders where they focus in on the most important task only to lose sight of all that is going on around them. It is important to have that wider perspective and to have 360-degree vision to see where you are, where you are going, and what is going on around you. How is your team doing? What about your competition, the marketplace, and the public that you are serving? A leader needs to have that 360-degree perspective.

A lighthouse, by design, also magnifies the light. One of the features that make a lighthouse so interesting is the lengths that their light can shine out into the distance. That is something that applies to us as leaders, as well. We have to be able to magnify the light that is within us, for leadership really comes from inside ourselves. One of the reasons that executive coaching is effective for professional development is that we explore with you what is inside you.

What are your resources, gifts, abilities, strengths, and experiences that you can bring to your leadership? How can you use all that you are to enhance your team? Your leadership will be magnified through the team that surrounds you. The message you are communicating is not just your voice, but is your voice echoed and magnifying through all of the other people who are part of your organization. It is all part of having a great vision, a good sense of your corporate myth, a good story that is motivating your company so that people have bought into it and really live it.

When the storms happen, you need the self-assurance that you will endure the wind and the waves. Leaders prefer to lead in the good times when all is bright and cheery. If it is a fair time, enjoy it! For most leaders in a world of rapid change, gentle days do not typically last. Cycles of the larger world economy and challenges in specific industries mean that there will be change and disruption that competition and disruption create.

Leaders expect that it is only a matter of time before they too will face the storm. Be prepared within yourself and within your organization to weather any storms that may come. Wherever they may come from, we have to be ready for them and know how to endure them.

The lighthouse needs maintenance. Back in the old days, it was the lighthouse keeper's role to ensure that the light was put on and always functioning through storms to serve the people who need that light. The outside needs painting from time to time. Repairs inside keep everything safe and functioning well. Like the lighthouse, leaders need maintenance, too. It helps when leaders invest the time to develop themselves as individuals and as leaders. They need time for refreshment in their family life, recreation, creativity and spirituality so that they can come to work with extra energy and the ability to make a difference in the community.

That is one of the key roles that executive coaches provide: they are there for you to give you that outside perspective. It is a point of view that is supportive of you and takes into account all of the things that are important to you as well as those priorities and goals for the organization that you are serving.

The lighthouse warns of danger. Leaders have to be the ones who can sense risks and warn of dangers ahead to ensure that we are prepared to avoid those dangers where we can.

When we think of lighthouses, we think of the word "light." Light is one of those things that do not seem very important when it is a bright, sunny day. Often leaders are not noticed during good times. Everything is moving along fine, people are meeting expectations, the stock market is going up, and the dividends are being paid; the expectations and earnings are there and are being met. It then seems like anyone can do it.

However, if you are in the dark of night or in a cloudy environment or an imminent storm, that is when you need the lighthouse to be at its brightest, and that is when it shines the most. That is when a leader has to show the qualities of their leadership, the strength of character and the courage that leaders need to face those difficult days.

That light of hope has to be there so that people can have confidence that they can weather the storm. When times are tough, the economy is difficult and careers are on the line, that is when leaders need to lead in a way that provides hope for the people they are serving.

For a community, a lighthouse is a positive influence. It is always there, showing the way. That is reassuring for someone at sea, in the harbour or on the land. Leaders have this positive influence, as well. Influential leaders have a balance between accomplishing the tasks while providing a high degree of support for the people in the organization and those they are serving. They strive to give their very best each and every day to make that organization and all the people within it successful so that the people of that organization are served well.

If you want to lead your world, you have to be a positive influence. The *influence* part is just as important as the *positive* part. It is not enough just to be a positive person with no influence; you need to be truly influential in creating change and creating possibilities for your organization to reach its potential. You will find that the positive influence is something that is valuable no matter where or when you are in the history of your organization.

So, the next time you see a lighthouse in a picture or if you happen to drive by one, think of that as part of your calling to be a great leader. Let your light shine through in the good times as well as the dark times so that the people you serve will have confidence that they will survive and thrive each and every day together.

WHO ARE THEY?

Being a leader would be so much easier if we had a team of "me, myself and I" at our disposal. If the task is a big one, we might even settle for our own version of the *Star Wars* Clone Army.

One of the temptations for a leader is to fall into the trap of believing that I not only know what's best, but can also do everything better than anyone else. That is usually quickly followed by the logical extension: therefore, I should do everything I possibly can do. This is not to say that you are not the most knowledgeable person on your team. Your skill may indeed be superior to everyone else in your group. But no leader should be fooled into thinking they can or should do it all.

A further extension of this "clone me now" thinking is a hiring strategy that tries to find more of you with your knowledge, skills and temperament. You might settle for younger than you if you can see that glimmer of yourself when you were newly minted in that prospect. Rarely do organizations need more people identical to us. That is because each role in a business or government department requires a different set of technical, administrative, sales or creative skills. It is also true that there are certain personality types that thrive in certain types of jobs. Assign the wrong communication style or type of personality to a role that does not fit and expect to hear a constant grinding sound.

There are many reasons to have a great human resources or employee relations department in an organization. More than setting up employment packages and working on benefits, a major function of the HR world is to assist leaders in defining the requirements of each position, understanding what kind of candidate would be ideal, and then interviewing and testing the recruits to make the best possible match.

The team will not be a happy or effective one if the wrong person is in the role. Customer service will deteriorate. Productivity will suffer. Profitability will drop.

If the right personality type with the right experience and commitment is selected, then the opposite is true. All the outcomes are different when a person fits their role in the team.

What qualifications are required? You and your team can identify the tasks and responsibilities for each position. The job description can outline the duties quite clearly. The posting can list the relevant skills and education required. But before you post that position, establish what type of personality is best suited for the role.

When I go into organizations as an executive coach or for seminars on topics like team building, I sometimes identify a problem with the fit between the person and the position. The result is anxiety, lack of motivation, conflict and a very unhealthy workplace. It usually comes down to the wrong personality type or communication style for what the position requires. The employer is unhappy. The employee is miserable. The customers are angry.

We have all experienced these corporate misfits. Meet the receptionist who dislikes people. Try to get clear instructions from the creative person who can explain something ten ways and does. Good luck to get something different done by the person who only can follow the rules. Ever try to get a payroll done on time by someone who would rather be talking to the friend in the other department?

It is so much easier to avoid a hire of the wrong person than to try to change your mind once they are on board. Even with probationary periods for evaluation, having the wrong person in the role often costs training time and money as well as lost productivity and tensions in the group where he or she is serving.

What can you do? Identify what kind of personality best suits the position being offered. Then add the usual kind of qualifications, education and experience that is needed.

Understand that in the need for a job or through a lack of self-awareness, many people cannot self-identify their own personality type. That is why using tools like personality tests is invaluable. Once you have candidates to consider, you can use communication styles and personality tests to give you additional information about the candidate. That, along with the other criteria that you already use, will improve your ability to make a good match for what you know the position will require.

As much as we feel like we are helping someone by giving them a job, the wrong job for that person is no gift. Their work that could be a fulfilling and rewarding part of life will sooner than later become something they despise and regret. On some level, they often blame the employer for hiring them and making them miserable. It is also much more painful for them to be terminated from a job than to not be hired in the first place.

As a leader, you will have enough challenges leading the team you inherit. Be sure that as people are added to the team they are not just qualified for the job, but their personality will shine through their work because it is a great fit for them and you.

So, be sure to know not only what you need but who they are when you hire a prospect. Everyone will thank you for it eventually.

YOUR INHERITANCE

Unless you are an entrepreneur who starts up a company or group, you are someone who will receive a bequest when it comes to your team. Your predecessor has left you a team and an organization at some point in its story. That is your inheritance.

Some leaders will leave you a healthy team who are in good form and are achieving great results for the challenges they face. Like receiving a million dollars from the will of a distant aunt or uncle, it is wonderful news.

Other leaders leave behind a dysfunctional team who do not know what they are doing or where they are going. Such a team is usually chaotic, occasionally angry and always in need of attention. That is more like being the executor for someone who left nothing but massive debts with many angry creditors to settle down. No fun at all!

Often the group is somewhere in between. Some aspects of the team are going well while others are not. How do you begin to pick up where your predecessor left off?

It helps to begin with some humility. At some point in the future, you will be the predecessor leaving the organization behind. Some who follow may feel that you have not done all the things you might have to leave the group in tip-top shape. You do not yet know all of the dynamics of the group that may have created instability or frustration for the previous leader and their plans.

Some of the people who are most delighted to see your predecessor leave are the most enthusiastic to see you come. They will tell you in whispered words all of many failures of the leader who is now history. Often they will also have some additional warnings for you about colleagues who ought not to be trusted.

Experienced leaders know that those who were anxious for your predecessor's transition out will likely be the ones celebrating your departure down the road. They are often people who dislike or are unwilling to work with leaders of any kind. They hope that you will be more pliable and cooperative with their worldview than the last one. Once they find out that you are a competent leader who will hear all sides and then move forward, they may sour on you, too. Then you become the target.

Instead, try to get a well-rounded picture of the present situation along with all of the "assets and liabilities" that are there to manage on your team. Get a sense of where the group has been and where they were heading.

Do your own evaluation of the information you receive. Understand that some will have their own agenda to try to control your decisions or advance their position. Try to connect with people on multiple levels to ensure that you are not just hearing the leadership perspectives. If you report to someone above you, ask questions to understand the story as well as their expectations for the future.

Change is a wonderful thing, but it can be particularly troubling for people who value continuity and predictability. Some new leaders enter a new role and want to immediately put their mark on the organization. They have bold initiatives that will be implemented immediately. Enough waiting. Let's go.

That works well if there is a strong consensus for the kind of change you are leading. Even then, you need to spend more energy and time than you would think necessary to allow for not just the goals and the objectives to be clear but for the process to work itself through. Many new leaders defeat themselves early by approaching a new role without assembling the followers. Like the train engine that is sailing down the tracks without the passenger cars, you will defeat the purpose of the change if you do not bring your team along with you intellectually, socially and emotionally.

Share with them your ongoing assessment of where you are and where you hope to go. Identify the challenges they are likely to face on the journey. Build up their self-confidence and preparation to ensure they, too, are equipped.

Time spent understanding the team's past, along with a thoughtful plan that is paced to the group's future, is key. Having the team own the plan will give you a better beginning with your new group. It will also prepare a nice inheritance for your successor!

BOO!

Everyone has fears. Remember the classic *Indiana Jones* moment where Harrison Ford's says, "I hate snakes!" even as they were all hissing around him at the bottom of the pit?

As a group of individuals, every team has members with fears. Some fears are related to common triggers like spiders and heights. Other fears are intangible and even more debilitating for the workplace, like a fear of rejection or a fear of failure. How does a leader help your team face their fears?

Fear will rob your team of energy and the willingness to stretch out to meet the needs of other team members, customers and clients. It is still a fearful time in most business cultures. Downsizing, outsourcing, financial collapse, corporate collapse, pension changes, benefit cutbacks and uncertainties of all kinds weigh heavily on people's emotions.

At the heart of the fears is also the rate of change. People can gradually handle change and absorb its good and bad. So much has changed in manufacturing and service jobs that it is difficult for people to see a future that appeals to them. Add to that generations who have been given the notion that you can be paid very well for little work, little education and little risk. Those traditional jobs have either seen massive cuts in pay and benefits or they have disappeared to more competitive and flexible countries. It stabs at their hearts, causing distraction and distress.

Not all fears are bad. We should be afraid of putting our hand into a fire. It is good that we have a fear of eating spoiled food. Many fears, however, are not helpful. They can keep us up at night or cause us to distrust others. Fears are the enemy of faith. Fear will cancel our confidence and have us unable to act in our best interests.

One of the things you can do as a leader is to help team members face their fears. That may mean bringing people in to help give people an opportunity to vent their fears and to express them. Certain personality types and communication styles are more prone to fear the future and dwell on all that could go wrong. Those team members especially benefit from your commitment to manage change carefully and thoughtfully as much as it is up to you.

Acknowledging our genuine fears is also healthy. It gives us the freedom that happens in a dark room when we turn on the light. There may be a boogeyman in the room, but having the light on ensures that you know where he is. Most things that we fear tend to disappear when we face them.

Understanding that a team is committed to the welfare of other members is helpful when facing some of life's grim realities. The important message that a leader can share with her or his team during a stressful time comes down to a very small word with powerful energy – that is the word "with." Humans usually do better facing their fears together. If they know that the leader and the team are committed to being with them through the ups and downs, they will be able to relax and focus on what can be done rather than on what may go wrong.

The same is true for the leader, as well. One of the values of having an executive coach is to know that there is someone there who is willing and able to walk along the journey with you. No matter how dark the road, we all need to know that someone is with us. That applies to family and friends, too. People of faith find comfort in that message as well as they experience the ups and downs of the human experience.

So the next time you have that fearful feeling creeping up slowly behind you, turn around and say, "Boo!" and you may find there was nothing there for you or your team to fear after all.

SHOTS FIRED

Sooner or later, as a leader you are going to be under fire. It might be the result of a bad decision you made. It could be the work of the "loyal opposition" who believe it is their duty to attack you whenever and wherever (not unlike Cato and the dear Chief Inspector Clouseau whenever Clouseau returned home). Sometimes you are the target because of the nature of your company and its mandate. You might be someone in charge of a division that is not performing up to expectations and senior management is shaking the chain of authority.

There might be an honest difference of opinion on the direction you are leading. You might be under fire from people outside of your group. Maybe it is the clients or the public. Often it is the result of disgruntled people in the organization who are unhappy with decisions that were different than they would have made. Some people do not like us. Sadly, sometimes others are just in a bad mood and they choose to take it out on you.

Part of being a leader is to expect to be under fire. Do not let anyone tell you otherwise. The leaders with the greatest minds, biggest hearts and boundless hope still faced unhappiness in their followers. Sometimes it is very painful. You are trying to do your best with an attitude of service and still they criticize. It becomes a real test of character when you hear the arrows go zipping by.

As leaders, we will offend people because, as former Prime Minister Tony Blair said well, "To decide is to divide." Choosing a course of action means that one or more alternatives were not taken. That can be a source of competition and criticism from others.

If you are new to leadership and you are experiencing your first round of criticism, it is okay to wince and duck as the attacks begin. It is part of being human. What does happen, thankfully, is that we build up a tolerance for it over time. If we can survive it long enough, we will build up an immunity to our unreasonable critics. While leaders rarely achieve superhero status where the attacks of others just bounce off our indestructible selves, most leaders do get used to the sound of the disgruntled.

Reading the biographies of great leaders can be reassuring to us as we face the complaints of those we try to serve. Even back in Biblical times, no less a leader than Moses, who led the people out of Egypt, heard more than his share of murmuring. In some seminars, I will ask the audience to start repeating the word "murmur" over and over. It is as disturbing as fingernails on the chalkboard after a while.

Even as we become less unsettled by criticism, a wise leader takes the time to hear their critics for any element of truth that might be there. It can serve to check our motives and our methods. How could we have done better? Sometimes our most vicious critics do us an unintended favor. They help us lead better next time. (Be sure to thank them when you can; it creates a great deal of disequilibrium that can be amusing to watch!)

What helps you stay true to your decisions is when you can say that the choices made were in the best interests of other people and done in the best way we know how. (Both are important; the right thing done the wrong way can undo the trust needed to make it happen.) If you have done your best, then you live with the consequences with a sense of integrity.

That does not always mean that the results are great. There are times when your division is going to miss the targets because of factors out of your control. Some who complain will never be satisfied. Others may envy your job and not give up until they have it. (If they only knew what it is really like, they might not be so anxious to have it!)

This is another case where it is important to exercise our power to forgive, detailed elsewhere in the book. Forgiving others who attack us without just cause is something we can choose to do to release ourselves from the anxiety and bitterness that comes from holding it in.

Where we have failed or made choices we regret, the best solution is to admit that and try to be reconciled to those we have offended. They may or may not accept our efforts and apology. What they choose to do is their problem. What we choose to do is about who we are and want to be.

That allows us to move forward being the best leader we can be. As the cabinet secretaries and others in the West Wing like to say, "I serve at the pleasure of the president." Those who called us to serve can remove us sooner or later as they choose to do so. Our job is to try our best to never make that a firing for cause.

So the next time you hear the sounds of thundering guns in the distance, do not lose heart. Take it as a backhanded compliment. It means they know you are the leader.

SHOOTING THE RAPIDS

We live in stressful times in business, government and the not-for-profit sector. Pressures from the economy and the rapid rate of change have led to more conflict and tension in the workplace. Gone is the quiet paddle down the river with a gentle current. Leaders now need to know how to navigate the rapids and hazardous currents in the workplace while keeping team members from going overboard. How can you shoot the rapids with your team without going down with the ship or canoe?

The answer is a commitment to team building. In many organizations, team building is now understood as a daily requirement for leaders so that the team can not only finish the journey but finish it together. The stresses of life at work and home can easily distract a team when dangers are present.

The reason that teams need to be constantly rebuilt is that when you put people in proximity to each other (even virtually!), there will eventually be conflict. Rather than team building, I sometimes call it "team patching" since most teams sustain some damage each and every day.

You don't have to look far or long at any set of relationships to find conflict as that's actually part of the human condition. To have conflict is to be human and to be human is to have conflict, it seems. Not all conflict is bad, of course. Conflict can be a very positive thing as it forces us to reexamine ourselves and our assumptions. Negative conflict, however, can damage and scar relationships and make teams fly apart if not addressed.

As much as it is uncomfortable for us when there is conflict, we should not be surprised. It is a reflection of the many differences that go into each and every one of us as individuals. Even if you imagine a world that only contained clones of only one of us, I think we recognize that the clones would have conflict too since we are all conflicted as individuals.

Conflicts can follow us from home to work and work to home. Like a virus, a conflict can spread as others are exposed to it. Eventually, the relationships become so tangled it will take a great deal of energy and time to sort out the conflict.

Every summer as waterfront director of a children's camp, I would open up the boathouse on Lake Huron. There I could reliably expect to discover the many lines and buoys of the swimming area casually tossed into the storage area by those who closed up the previous summer. Clearly the ropes had spent the winter months entangling themselves like some kind of cruel puzzle for us to solve. Out on the sandy beach, the group of waterfront staff would sit in a huge circle trying to untangle some part of the maze before us. (For those of you who fish, you understand the challenge on a smaller scale as fishing lines are also very crafty and devious, seizing any and every opportunity to tangle into knots.)

It took both patience and time for us to start untangling these lines so that they could once again return to mark the swimming area in the lake. Ignoring the small tangles that were beginning to happen in August as the ropes were pulled out led to a great waste of time in June.

The little issues that are not handled early on when a conflict appears usually require many more resources to resolve if left alone. For leaders, the challenge is how to minimize the negative effects of conflicts.

Similarly, knowing the difference between what is urgent and what is important will define how effective you are as a leader. Many organizations spend their energies responding to the many urgent matters and people who are always present to consume their time. Wise leaders help their team set an agenda that creates a sense of urgency toward the things that are truly important. Governments, not-for-profit organizations and businesses that do not commit sufficient resources to doing the job well will always be vulnerable to the tyranny of the urgent. That can create a death spiral of unmet commitments and disappointed clients.

This is especially true in customer service, where a structure that only responds to complaints will never improve. Only when customer service is proactive in learning of problems before the customer comes to complain will it be effective in the long term. One approach tries to protect the company, while the other is designed to truly serve the customer. That takes sufficient resources to succeed.

Do not allow someone else's urgent to become your urgent unless you know that it is also important.

Some leaders choose to ignore conflict out of a fear that intervention will only make matters worse or that it is not important enough to take our focus. Others take a sledgehammer to any hint of conflict, assuming that fear of discovery will drive conflict away. What we know is that conflict left alone tends to grow and infect a larger circle as those in the conflict seek allies to support their view of the war.

This topic, like so many for leaders, is about modeling for those on your team how to deal with each other in a positive way when conflict does occur. Leaders can model how to engage others when there is a conflict to resolve the differences. Note that the word here is "resolve," not "eliminate." "Resolve" suggests that we come to terms with the differences that are there. We rarely can eliminate the differences. What we can show is how to acknowledge our differences and then continue to move forward even with those differences.

Beyond resolving the conflict, leaders can also demonstrate how to value each member of the team regardless of the differences we all bring to the equation. You can acknowledge the conflict and then encourage each party to give the other the benefit of the doubt. If someone becomes a constant source of conflict, then you can address that person directly to discover what the underlying issues are and how to lead them back to teamwork rather than sabotage.

Often those involved in repeated and seemingly petty conflict have a problem with forgiveness. That deserves its own chapter, which will follow next.

HAIL TO THE CHIEFS

On a visit to Washington, D.C., I had the opportunity to meet a United States Navy chief petty officer where I was staying. As I usually do, I was interested to learn about his career and what his life was like as a chief. During the conversation, I learned about an interesting leadership tradition in that branch of the service. It is called the charge book or sometimes the log book.

The chief petty officer is the beginning of the top class of rank of the enlisted men and women in the Navy. The equivalent in the Air Force is the master sergeant and above; the Marines have the gunnery sergeant, while in the Army it is called a sergeant first class.

In the Navy, moving from the rank of petty officer to a chief petty officer represents an important promotion. The Navy has a proud tradition, as do the other services. Promotions are one of those times when commitments kept are honored. While leadership is expected at all levels of service, the chief positions correctly describe the senior nature of the position.

As the most experienced sailors, the chief petty officers have separate quarters from the other sailors. The chiefs' quarters are known as "The Goat Locker," reflecting either the tradition of keeping the milk animals safe on long voyages in bygone days or perhaps because the more senior men might be called the "old goats" as a nickname.

The charge book or log book was traditionally used to record the various events that took place on a ship's voyage. The book might include some of the routine tasks or great adventures, like battles at sea. More than just a diary, these books were also to include what was learned through the experiences as well as the factual accounts. This was a way of continuing to benefit from what you had experienced in addition to knowing the accounts from the trip.

The chief told me that a candidate for promotion to chief was to use every opportunity they could to approach a navy chief they might meet in their duties or on leave. During the encounter, the candidate would ask the chief to tell him something he should know from the chief's many experiences.

As part of the mentoring process, each chief is ready with stories, principles, and lessons learned from their experience over the years. Some of these stories might reflect a positive outcome. Other stories might have been difficult failures. Through the many encounters, the prospective leaders would assemble a charge book full of lessons to follow or to avoid to further prepare them for their own leadership experiences as a chief. The quality and volume of the log book would be included in the evaluation of the readiness for the candidate for promotion to the elite class of naval servicemen and women, the naval chief.

The senior leaders were ready with stories to tell.

The candidate was ready to learn.

This is a useful model for leaders outside of the service, as well.

One of the reasons that the chiefs share a commitment to teaching the candidates how to lead is that the chiefs all play a key role in the well-being of everyone on that vessel. An ill-prepared chief could put everyone at risk. There is also a pride of rank that wants each chief to live up to the great ideals of that tradition.

The process also reminds the up-and-coming leaders of the value of learning from those who have gone before them. That creates an atmosphere where leaders remain teachable. Too often leaders believe mistakenly that they have arrived and do not need any further input. That is a dangerous place to be.

Different than mentoring one-on-one, this proud tradition is a helpful model to remind each leader of the opportunity and obligation to pass along their stories of conquest and failure so the next generation is better prepared to face the battles that will surely come.

Find a leader you know and ask her or him to tell you something you should know from their experience. As a leader, be ready to be asked!

DID YOU BRING THE PLAYBOOK?

The hardest thing for a team is to know where it is how well their plan will work out. Every team in sports like baseball, football, or soccer wants to win. They aspire to be the champions or at least to exceed expectations! They are willing to work toward that. Some teams win, and some teams lose. Why?

The same group of individuals can be successful one year and terrible the next. There are certainly intangibles that are difficult to define that can cause a team to jell and at other times slump badly. Often, however, it comes down to playbooks. Notice that I use the plural here because in sports it is not only what you plan to do, but also how your opposition plays their game.

A team in soccer with an outstanding winger is Tottenham Hotspurs' Gareth Bale. As he matured in his game, he could dazzle teams in England's Premier League and in Europe. His amazing acceleration, combined with his ability to cross the ball into areas where goals could be scored, gave his team a great advantage. After a year of owning many of the defenders he faced, the opposition adjusted by double-teaming him and placing faster defenders to cope with his speed and skill. That changed the game for Spurs. Tottenham then had to adjust by having Bale play a more central role or switch sides during play to create opportunities.

Whatever your playbook says, it is only as good until the game starts. Then you must adjust as the opposition brings its game to you.

Does the fact that your playbook will need to change make it unnecessary? Not at all. Is it pointless to run your plays and drills in training knowing that it might not line up against one of more teams? Of course not. You need to have a playbook that becomes the basis for your team play. Then the coach or leader has to know how to adjust to the changing flow of the game as these two teams encounter each other.

Leaders need to have a clear sense of how to use the human resources represented on their teams. What are the talents on your team? Who is good at what? Who is best at something? Who can fill in for a position if the main person doing that role is away or unable to continue?

Effective leaders take the time to know their team members so that they can do the things that encourage the best performances from each and every member of the group.

The value added comes when the leader can add some inspiration to the group's perspiration. People can go through the motions and get the job done. Top-performing groups have leaders who can inspire their teams to exceed expectations by adding the intangibles that leaders can share. Those are things like confidence, encouragement, challenges and rewards that help the team members know that they are on a mission together.

The coach and the manager set the tone and give them a sense of direction. What can you do to build the team in the right direction? How can you ensure that the team has the same vision of where you are going and why you are going where you are going? Give them the opportunity to buy into it and to own the process that you are going through. This does not mean that they need to know every little plan, but they should all understand the big ideas for the team to use. Have a playbook that is well prepared with a team that is ready to succeed.

POSITIVE PERSUASION

"The arguments are often cumulative in nature and not individually persuasive." This was one of the many memories of listening to the great professor, Dr. Norman R. Ericson of Wheaton College.

You might need to reread that quote a time or two to get the full impact of what he was saying. It has important implications for not only our thinking but our leadership, as well.

Leaders are in the business of moving individuals and groups forward to conquer the challenges ahead. Some that we lead will be happy just to know the instructions that are to be followed. Others find a destination chosen as sufficient motivation to move forward. But many that you will lead are not going to move far or for long without being convinced.

As a leader, that usually means that we want to give them the one big reason for them to do something. That should be enough, and then they should just get moving. Yet, many times there are no obviously grand arguments to convince a group of what is to be done. That could be because the destination is shrouded in time or distance and therefore difficult for everyone to visualize. Other times, there may appear to be several equally valid decisions that could be made, and so those we lead will be uncertain that the one we announce is necessarily the best one.

This can be very frustrating for the leader who is confident of the direction to go but is experiencing resistance from her or his team members. The temptation is to try to give them "the big reason" that should be convincing and sufficient. Often there is no one reason that is so clear that everyone will instantly agree. It is usually more complicated than that. Absent an ultimate argument, we are tempted to blend authority with argument to create an ultimatum. We end up saying unhelpful things like "I am in charge here; we will do what I say," or that other tried-and-true hammer, "I know what is best. If you do not like it, lump it." We revert to tactics that frustrated parents use with their challenging preteens. The results are often just as poor. We have traded our opportunity to persuade with the easier choice to control those we serve as leaders. That is not the best way to effect change as executives.

Unless it is truly a crisis, most people in most cultures do not like to be controlled. We resist those expressions of control where we do not have a choice in our behaviors. Think of how most people feel and act when they are in a line, for an easy example.

If there is an emergency situation, however, these same people are willing to do what first responders or those in authority tell them to do. We are willing to rely on their training and judgment to manage the crisis to maximize safety and minimize risk.

Note that once the crisis has passed, these same people are quite willing to criticize the conduct of those handling the crisis if not done well. That willingness to trust the authorities fades as quickly as the perception of the crisis. If the authorities try to exert control beyond the urgent period where it is required, they will face growing opposition.

Leaders need to be very careful not to play the crisis card unless it truly is one. Rarely is there only one course of action. It is unusual that action must be taken instantly in most businesses or groups you will lead. Leaders, however, are tempted to escalate problems to a crisis level to trigger a faster response by their group members. It does not take long before the team members see through this. They can tell the difference between a Chihuahua and a wolf no matter what the leader calls it. Leaders who over-control lose two key elements of the effective leader that are interconnected: credibility and trust.

This brings us back to the Dr. Ericson quote. Most often, leaders will have to persuade their followers through a series of facts and issues rather than one big argument that tips the decision all by itself. It is the cumulative nature of a series of smaller facts and arguments that must be considered. Taken together, this creates a wise course of action. As much as that can seem like the slow way to achieve results, it is the way that will keep the leader's credibility and the trust of those they lead.

Obviously, the leader only needs to assemble the facts and arguments to the level that is helpful to moving the team and its members forward in the change required. Most of the team will not insist on much information most of the time. That is especially true when the leader is trusted. But if there is hesitation or resistance, the leader should be able to assemble the facts and implications to make the argument in a way that is persuasive.

Another part of effective persuasion is our use of learning channels. Very simply, most people learn best by seeing, hearing or doing. More formally, these ways of learning are called visual, auditory or kinesthetic. Some people are a combination of two best channels to learn, while others can learn equally well by all three. Think of these as frequencies on a radio. If you do not set the broadcast on the frequency they are receiving, your message will not get through. For an email example, if you do not use their exact email address, do not expect them to know what you thought you shared.

What is your preferred learning channel? Did you study for a test by reading the words? Did you learn better by hearing the teacher or someone else review it with you? Did you have to write something down or do something with the information to learn it well? These and many other cues tell us what learning channel or frequency is best for us. This is also true of those who work with us too.

If you are share your communications to the team in writing, some people may not really absorb that well while others will prefer it. Some will do well if you share your instructions orally rather than writing it down. You may find that some in your group do best with step-by-step instructions that they then carry out. If you find that people do not understand your communication, explore whether their learning channel might be something different from what you are using. The best group communication assumes that in our team, we will have all three learning channels. If the message is important, you might want to share it in a meeting by speaking it, demonstrate the steps by having others show it, and follow up with a written memo that reviews the instructions. Covering all three learning channels works best for all of us, no matter which channel is our strongest one. How you communicate is part of your persuasion strategy.

Organizations often contain "the loyal opposition" who feel it is their duty to oppose any and every initiative. Leaders need to be confident enough in their recommendations and decisions to be able to overcome those self-appointed guardians of the status quo.

That can be a positive outcome when there is opposition or hesitation. Leaders should especially take note when those who usually follow easily suddenly resist. There may be a flaw in the plan that they know or sense. Sometimes in the restating of the argument, the leader may hear some other perspectives that might improve the decision. Effective leaders are open to new information and better decisions while there is a window to do so.

What that commitment to persuasion and influence shows the team members is that they are respected. That respect creates a bond between team members and the leader. Leaders with that kind of positive influence achieve much more than those who take the shortcut of control.

BRIDGES

When it comes to being a positive influence in your world, one of the key ideas as a leader is being able to sell yourself. Your leadership includes being able to earn the trust and commitment of your team. Yes, they may and should accept you as their leader simply because you have been appointed to the role. That may work for a while, but ultimately they will only truly engage all of their talents and energy for the team if they buy into you as a leader.

In the United States, the term "bully pulpit" speaks to one of the intangible powers of the president. The president can use his (or someday her!) powers of persuasion to challenge the nation to move toward or away from a policy or cause. Throughout history, it may be the most potent tool in that very powerful office. Presidents who were able to move the country forward through good and bad times had the confidence of the people of the country. Even those who may not agree with the political agenda or party affiliation of the leader might be persuaded to buy into the policy if the president was sufficiently powerful with their message.

In contrast, weak presidents are often characterized by an inability to persuade others of their policies. The persuasion might be in speeches but often also includes developing effective relationships where the legislators and others are willing to negotiate and follow.

Ultimately, the wisdom and effectiveness of the policy and its implementation becomes the measure of whether the country will continue to follow their leader's vision and plans. But if the leader can be persuasive, they earn the right to try. Many leaders with great ideas never have their plans tested because they could not convince others to buy into their leadership. They did not make the sale.

This is another place where knowing who you are as a person and a leader is foundational. There are many things that shape us and our worldview. Our parents, education, generation, and many more factors color our way of looking at life. What is important in selling ourselves is to take who we are and reach out with that to others. We essentially have to build communication bridges to others who are the same as and different from us. As with bridge building, you start on your side and reach over the divide to the other side.

Great leaders can build those bridges in all directions. Older can inspire younger. Younger can reassure older. Democratic blue can turn Republican red to at least purple for the moment. Republican can convince Democrat that they should at least give the other side a chance to try it. Within any nation there are so many divides it is amazing that the nation-state lasted this long. Bridge-building leaders are usually responsible for the periods in which good things happen. Sometimes that is because government was involved. Other times, it was because government got out of the way. Effective leaders know what is needed when and how to communicate that to others.

Ultimately, bridges only have value if people actually use them to cross between where they are and where they might be. Leaders have to be willing not just to build the bridge but to cross it and to extend the invitation to others to cross back to the leader's side, as well.

When you are selling yourself as leader, people respond to authenticity. That is another reason why knowing and being yourself is essential to reaching out to others to follow. In politics, those who would lead have to ask others to vote for them. If enough people are willing to give that trust through their vote, the leader has the opportunity to begin or continue to lead.

Unless you are in politics or a position that is elected, it is likely that you are leading because someone hired, appointed or promoted you to the position. You may have asked for the position, or perhaps you were asked to take on the challenge.

As leader in most business or government settings, you will not be asking those on your team for their vote. But make no mistake—they will vote on your leadership regularly by cooperating with or hindering what you are trying to accomplish. Most companies include performance reviews that include the feedback of the team members.

You cannot truly mentor a large team. What you can do is mentor the leadership team that is part of your inner circle. Equip them to be great leaders. Give them the strong support and clear expectations that will enable them to give their best. Then help them to mentor their smaller team by giving them not only the example of mentoring but the underlying principles and practices that help leaders pass along their knowledge and experience too. That is how leaders multiply themselves as well as their bottom line.

Earning the continuing trust of your team comes with your ability to lead well. But it starts with your ability to sell yourself to them as a leader who is committed to their success and the success of the others in the group.

Start building those bridges. Be sure to inspect them regularly to ensure that your connection to each team member is strong.

ON THE BOIL AND ON THE WOBBLE

Like all teams, you are going to have winning streaks and you are going to have losing streaks. What you need to do is to prepare for success, but stand by for whatever else happens. That is one of the realities of working in any government organization or company, or even in a volunteer group. Your best plans are always subject to change, and that is because you are dealing with people.

Team members go through different experiences in their home that affect their job. Colleagues go through health issues, friendship issues, and other things that affect their job. Many things happen that are going to affect the job. That is not including the variables of the economy, government programs, elections, and the more subtle things that affect what is going on.

Consequently, be flexible and ensure that your group is focused on being an effective team. If your team is good, then you have people with the right skill sets working in the right place and you are maximizing their potential. You can be confident. You will adapt. Your team will adapt because the team itself is strong and capable.

Find some other coaches in your organization. You may notice that in many teams you might have a general manager and then maybe a head coach. In football you would have an offensive coach, a defensive coach, and coaches that work with special teams. There is lots of coaching going on. The reason that is necessary is that there are so many different roles to play.

Similarly, while you may be the official leader of the group, make sure that you are finding other people to lead with you, as well. You have to put together that kind of energy that comes from many people, not just a single person, in order to have it affect your group. The larger your organization, the more team builders and encouragers you need. You want to nurture and develop those people who have the skills to identify the strengths in others. At the same time, they need to look at the weaknesses honestly then find constructive ways to minimize those challenges. Always, they are in encouragement mode. To encourage means to pass courage along so that it is in them. Encouragers make encouragement transferable. If you have those people in your organization, release them to engage the energy in your group. Your team will be strong.

As you learn about team building, you will notice that teams will change. Sometimes change is good. Those of us who love the Toronto Maple Leafs and hockey have been waiting for there to be a change back to the way it was in 1967, the last time the Toronto Maple Leafs won the Stanley Cup. Maybe you are a Boston Red Sox fan and you are so excited that finally the "Curse of the Bambino" is over with a World Series win.

Teams change. If you are on a losing streak, then that is really good news, but if you are a winner, then you might worry about that. That perfect moment when everything seems to be going well and the team seems to be working great might disappear. How is that going to affect your success?

As a team builder, prepare yourself for change. Most organizations actually need change to keep the organization strong. There are many change triggers. Sometimes it is age, with retirement forcing a change. Family moves and health changes can be the cause. Others may leave your organization because they have another challenge or opportunity they want to pursue.

When that happens, it is hard not to take it personally. "What did we do wrong? Didn't we have it going great here? Wasn't this the most amazing place to be? Why would you want to be anywhere else?" That is something that other people have to answer for themselves. Still, there will be these changes.

You may also find individuals in your group who just do not make it as a team player. These people may just be wonderful and outstanding individuals who cannot play on the team. You may have to say good-bye to certain individuals who, for the sake of the team, need to leave. You want to make that decision after you have given them an opportunity to see if you can work that person in to the group. Find where their strengths are put to the best use. Minimize the weaknesses that they bring to the equation. If you can make it work, that is great, because it is always harder to migrate new people into the team than to work with the ones who are there.

However, some people just will not learn. Usually because of their personality, these team members assume that they know and you do not. Sometimes it is a necessary decision to say good-bye to individuals. When those things happen, you want to adhere to the responsibilities that you have within the organization. Give them the opportunity to change to confirm that it is not about you. Document and do all of the things that are required by law or company policy.

When it comes time to let someone go, be clear with her or him about the positive things that they had brought to the organization. This is not being hypocritical or trying to soften the blow. It is simply trying to give that person something good too as they leave.

Early experiences in sports and places like a summer camp help individuals learn how to function successfully in a group, as well. As you are looking at your team members, explore some of their background experiences for clues. Do not be surprised that those who have opted for sports like tennis or were the soloist and not part of the choir will be strong individualists. Your team may need some who can go solo, but do not expect these people to play well in the sandbox.

This is true for any retail organization, as well. The most effective retail organizations are people-driven. They focus on customer service: How do we ensure that our customers get what they need quickly and at the best price?

Every organization in business, government, education or the community has to have that same commitment. If you do not have customer service central to your mission, you will not be successful.

To the degree you can help that environment to be positive and encouraging, you set the example as a team leader. The team leader serves the team. The team will value the importance of service, as well.

KNOWING YOUR MOTTO

One of the many interesting experiences in researching your family history is discovering your connection to not only past individuals but family groups, as well. If your roots are in countries that had clans or other family groups, this can add another piece of your family story. My roots are largely from Scotland with some Irish and English added for good measure. In the case of the Scottish people, they were organized many centuries ago into the clans that dominated regions of the country. The clan included many smaller family group names (septs) included in it, but each had a principal or leading family that gave their family its identity. Clans identified themselves by not only their name but their tartan (colors and patterns used in their clothing) and a coat of arms with images that spoke about the nature of the clan.

Mottos to further identify the clan (sometimes as a war cry) began in the 14th and 15th centuries and were more common by the 17th century.

The family crest was to act as a summary statement of what was characteristic of that clan. My Fairley family was part of the Rose clan, who have a nice red tartan. The harp was the symbol of the family, and our motto is "Constant and True." My wife is pleased to point out that her family roots are MacKenzies, who were the top family of their area having the clan name, along with some very fine dress and hunting tartans. Their clan motto is "Luceo non uro," translated as "I shine, not burn."

Mottos, like many other proverbs, slogans, mission statements or clichés, do not tell the whole story, but they are helpful. A motto is a way of summing up a purpose or characteristic of a person or group that is both descriptive and prescriptive. It should on some level describe what your team is about already. It should also prescribe what you want your group to be known for in the future, as well.

Leaders are constantly torn between the general and the specific. How much do we keep the ideas big and general so they apply as widely as possible? The flip side is to know how to make the big ideas translate into the everyday decisions being made.

Companies and governments go through many exercises to develop their mission statement to attempt to define the parameters of their activities and purposes. This can be useful as an exercise, but it is always a challenge to take a page of text and act upon it.

Just as Twitter has demonstrated the challenge and benefit of summarizing our thoughts into a bite-sized piece, coming up with a motto that is consistent with the organization's mission statement is helpful, too. It becomes something that everyone can own and use as a measure of how their activities and choices are consistent with that purpose statement or motto.

If your customers were creating a motto that describes your company or government department, what would they likely say? How does that compare to what you would like them to say? What would your team members say is the motto that describes the team at the moment? Is that where you want to be?

Go through the exercise of creating a motto that works as an inspiration for your team as well as a standard for each of the team and its leaders to use to measure the outcomes. Then keep it in front of the team regularly to move everyone to the goal of teamwork, productivity and customer service that you want to be characteristic of your group.

FIREFIGHTING

When there is conflict in your group, the temperature starts to rise within your team. Stress increases. Tempers get short. People brace for more uncomfortable moments. Everyone starts to feel the heat – and share the tension. Your group is wasting their emotional energy, and productivity will fall.

The battle is on. Solve it or risk the conflict escalating and spreading. You have to turn up the emotional air conditioning to try to cool everyone off.

That's not easy for many leaders. The temptation is to write it off to someone having a bad day, except that it has been more than just a day or even two. Often, by the time the leader is aware of the conflict, it has been growing between two individuals or between groups or departments for a while.

Firefighters are taught the importance of attacking the fire quickly. They want to be very careful and follow what they know about the tactics of fighting the fire to minimize the risk.

The one fact that gives them urgency, however, is the "two-minute rule." They know that a typical fire left to burn will double in size every two minutes. That means that it is twice the size at four minutes. By six minutes, it is four times bigger. By eight minutes, it is a fire that engulfs eight times the original size. By ten minutes, it is sixteen times what it was at two minutes. That difference between eight and ten minutes can be the difference between life and death for those trapped in a fire.

Leaders have to be prepared to attack the fires that they find smoldering in their organization. If ignored, these conflicts will turn to flame and spread well beyond where they began.

One of the root causes of many conflicts is the natural differences between the personality types in every group. An important part of team building is to train people become aware of who they are and then start to recognize people who are different and similar in personality to them. Once there is an appreciation that their differences are essential for the group to work successfully together, a new tolerance is created for what would be irritants otherwise. When people are understood to be acting as they are expected to do, it starts to put the fire out.

Often it takes the leader bringing the principals involved together to review not just the facts of the conflict but the communication styles involved, as well. This is not to excuse behavior that is inappropriate or that requires sanctions. But where the conflict is a result of minor irritations and personality, you can put those fires out by bridging the personalities involved.

I usually have the individuals explain their actions and relate it to their personality type or communication style. Then the other party does the same. Usually they are acting as you would expect their type of personality would be expected to act.

At that point it is helpful to review why certain behaviours tend to irritate the other type of personality. Each party needs to be reminded that while they may not have intentionally tried to offend the other person, they did not intentionally take steps to avoid it.

Sharing how to reach out to and work with each of the personality types and communication styles gives people a tool to reach beyond their typical way of interacting with the world. Just as learning to say a few words in a foreign language communicates to the listener that you respect them and their world, learning to reach across personality types helps, too.

Those efforts encouraged by the leader and modeled for their team will quench the fires that have been burning. It can be a value-added experience that not only stops the damage but makes the team stronger for the future.

Do not wait for the office fires to grow.

SITTING ON THE BENCH

Team members need to feel needed. They are content to spend some time on the bench if someone else is needed more for the team to succeed. However, no one wants to stay on the bench with the only prospect of play being when most of the rest of the team is injured. When you are on the bench too often or for too long, you no longer feel needed.

There is nothing that will destroy a team faster than being disconnected from the mission. If you are no longer needed, you are alienated. These negative feelings turn to apathy. Soon it will seep into the attitudes and thinking of the others on the team. One by one, many begin to feel like they are not needed. They conclude that it does not matter if I put my best into today. It does not matter if I am giving my all. If the message comes back that you are not needed, that person's energy will wither and die within the organization.

That is what often happens in organizations. If you have people who no longer feel valuable and valued, they will contaminate the rest of your group. They will intentionally or unintentionally undermine all sorts of other aspects of your organization, and your team will fall apart. Leaders can expect to be distracted by the feuding that will follow.

People need as part of regular evaluations (as well as in between those evaluations) to be told that they are valued and important. It is not just enough to say, "Hey, great to have you as part of the group. We are glad you are here." That is fine, but it is not enough. People need to know in detail *why* they are valued.

The more specific you can be as a team builder in giving people feedback, the more effective you are going to be in seeing the team grow and strengthen. If you can say to somebody, "You know, I really appreciate what you are doing with that customer. I was watching you, and I saw how you smiled at that customer. I saw how you looked him in the eye, and you really showed your concern for him. When there was a problem, you were patient with him and you listened to him, and you worked on it until you solved it. I really appreciate you being that careful and that committed to making that customer happy."

Provide those comments to your team members privately. As you give them that kind of feedback, they are going to be excited about their job. They will know that the effort they are making is valued not just for the work that gets done but because they are part of the team.

People feel valued when they receive that kind of feedback. That leads to an excitement about coming to work because they know that what they are doing is worthwhile.

Recent studies show that many of the professions that have the highest degree of burnout and job dissatisfaction are those in situations in which they are far away from feedback. In contrast, the professions and jobs that tend to be the most satisfying to people who do them are the ones in which they are getting more feedback from the client.

Roles like doctors and nurses and people in the teaching professions often have the best level of satisfaction with their job. It is not because of the work that they do—important as it is—but because they are getting feedback from the patient or from the client or student more regularly, and it is that feedback that gives people the extra energy to say, "Yes, I am going to do a good job again and again. My work matters. My life matters. My team matters." The same kind of principles apply when it comes to team building. You want to make sure that your team is getting feedback about how they are doing. They need to be receiving recognition and follow-up. Sharing specific examples of what they are doing well is a wise thing to do.

The professions that are starved for feedback are the ones involving people in research. The work that they are doing is very long and painstaking, often taking a long time for something to happen. Even when it happens, it is going to go for further testing. Years can pass before the results are confirmed. It is such a long time before someone is helped by the research that they did in the pharmaceutical or other industries.

Everyone needs to receive feedback all along the way. One of the things you need to do as a team builder is give regular and specific feedback so that people know that they are recognized. Good feedback not only includes what they do but values who they are as team members.

The ones most discouraged in the process may need the most feedback. Those who feel less necessary to the success of the organization need opportunities to not only contribute but to be recognized, too. Many leaders ignore their team members when things are going well. As a good mechanic will tell you, do not wait until the wheel is squeaking to oil it. Maintaining the emotional health of your team is something you should plan to do regularly.

A good coach ensures that all of the players get into the game sooner or later. Off the bench and into the game is when players can prove their worth or potential value to the team. Keep up your team's morale by keeping people in the game.

THE ONE AND THE MANY

As a leader who cares about having an effective team, you will inevitably ask the questions "How can I make the team that I have work the best? How can I make these people, a group of individuals, work together as a team well?"

It helps to recognize that one of the images you have as leader is that of a coach. Think about what great coaches have done for you in your sports or other group experiences. The best coaches deal with each of the players one-on-one as if they were the only member of the team. Yet, when the individuals need to work well together, the coach is able to motivate and choreograph each of the individuals to work smoothly together for the common good. Coaches, like all leaders, need to be able to work with the one and the many.

When we participate in a team-building seminar or work with leaders on managing their team, understanding the one and the many is one of the first stops on the journey.

Some of the people who are the greatest individual performers are the worst people when it comes to being on a team. Those who have some of the wonderful skills and talents are woeful team players. Those special abilities that make them great can lead them to a worldview that is very much a combination of "Me, myself and I." They can become convinced of their self-importance and indispensability. Whether it is in business, sports, sales or a family, people who stand out sometimes find it tough to play well with others. How the coach handles these "talents" will often make or break a team.

Baseball is one of those wonderful sports that allow us to understand this really well. Baseball is a team sport, and yet much of the game is spent being an individual. A pitcher throws the ball alone. The batter stands as an individual waiting to hit the ball. In the field, the shortstop waits to catch the ball. There is a team there, but much of the activity that is going on really is highly individualized.

This kind of organization requires people who will operate independently on the road, from home offices or from a variety of sites. Those team members need to be self-starters and reliable finishers. You want them to be able to be successful on their own, and together these many individual stars make up your team. They need you as their leader and coach to have excellent lines of communication with each of them individually along with ways to measure their progress and challenges.

In contrast, there is North American football, where there is action happening in many directions at once. It is a busy sport when the play is under way (then the long pauses to reset the lines…). You do have some individual play as the quarterback throws to the wide receiver for a catch, but the rest of the team is engaged in blocking or running alternative routes. A choreographed event happens every down. If the play goes according to plan, there are yards gained and points scored. They fail when one of more of the team members do not play their part or the other team played their part better.

If your model for an organization is more like football, your group functions better if people work cooperatively. Your team's success does not depend so much on individual achievements as much as the ability of your group to work comfortably and effectively together as they use their personal talents and skills. As the leader, you need to be aware of not only the individual performance of your team but also how well they are interacting with the others in the group. Where there are tensions, lack of communication or an unwillingness to work together, your team will lose energy. That energy loss will limit the potential of your team to reach the targets and possibilities that might be possible when everyone is working well together.

Different strategies feed these two types of teams. What they have in common is that the best teams maximize the person's strengths and minimize the person's weaknesses. So, no matter who they are and whether you prefer the baseball, tennis, football, soccer or hockey analogy, you want the team to succeed. That may require you to have many one-on-one connections to your team members who are spread out. Or you may need to be able to handle the group dynamics of working with team members who are playing together.

Either way, you are the coach who is there to move the team onto the field when needed, pull them off when they need a break, and coordinate their efforts so that the individuals and the team succeed.

CHEERS

Teams are great. Maybe your early team experiences were as the kid who was always picked first, or perhaps you were the kid that always got picked last. It does not matter because you are on a team right now.

In fact, you are probably on several teams. We are all in teams, and sometimes in many different teams in different areas of life. Sooner or later, we realize that we are on some team whether we like it or not.

Whatever team it is that you are on, you can make a difference. You can choose to be one of the people who will encourage the others on your team. Be the one who can identify the tasks and services that other people are doing well. Give them that feedback.

To earn their trust and their respect, the best principles to have working for you include the idea of making everyone on your team a success: "I want our team to be successful. I want the company to succeed, and I want to do the best for our shareholders or for the government. We want to serve the public well."

Whatever the category of customer or client you serve, it always comes down to what is best for that end user of your services or product. As a leader, you are there to assist others in being effective in their role on your team. Remember, these people working around you are creating their life story each day, just as you are.

How do you figure into their story? If their life were a movie, would you be the hero who helped them succeed or the villain who robbed them of the potential successes that they might have realized?

Another way to think of this is to consider the difference between a page and a chapter. To the leader, those on their team are like pages in the story. There might be five of them or one hundred pages. To the follower, there is usually only one main leader in their world. The typical leader is much more important in the life of the typical team member. Think back to grade 5. You might remember a great deal about your teacher and those days in her or his classroom. Who that teacher is, what they say or do not say to us and how they think about us is very important to us at that stage. They loom large in our lives. In contrast, we were one of perhaps twenty or thirty students in their class that year. They may have taught for twenty or thirty years. That is a great number of students for them to remember. Our teacher might be one of a dozen or so that were part of our years in elementary school.

The same effect can be seen with leaders in our story. The leader sees the ten or two hundred team members multiplied by the many teams they may lead over their career. Those who lead are often larger than life to the many team members. How a team member's day or week goes is heavily influenced by not only the decisions but by the tone set by their leader. If a team member feels that the leader walked by and ignored them, their day might be filled with doubt about whether they have offended or let down the boss. The leader, on the other hand, may have been walking to solve a problem, unaware of the team member they brushed past without a glance. Since leaders do play such a large role in the life of their team members, it is important to connect with the team members regularly so that they will feel affirmed and valued. Just as the history of a time is marked by who was the president or monarch during that period, your term of leadership will be remembered by those who serve with you as your years too. Make that not only a profitable and productive time but also one in which each team member felt valued and supported. Remember, they may be just one of many pages in your chapter, but you are a chapter in their story.

In the course of working for the company—whether it is for a year or two, five, or ten years, maybe long enough to get the gold watch—this is their life story. If you could help them reach their potential as individuals and as members of your team, you will have created a path to success for them that might not have been available without you.

That same commitment to individuals on your team strengthens your team together because there is a mutual bond created. When someone shows that they are willing to believe in us, invest in us and support us, we tend to rise to the occasion. We will be more likely to do that little extra that will better serve those in our story.

They can look back on their time with you as their team leader or as one of the members of the team and say, "Those were good times. Maybe business was tough, but we worked it out. We worked together as team, and we cared about each other."

That is a gift that you can give to anybody at any time on any team. It is great to be part of a team. You might as well get used to it: We are all parts of teams all of the time.

If you can take your team and continually encourage and challenge them, you will be a team builder. As a leader, you will be in demand. As people have the opportunity to reflect on their lives, they will come to value the approach you took to enable them to succeed.

Many people worry about their legacy as leaders. How will they be remembered?

What would you give to have a team who remembered you as someone who believed in them, trusted them and helped them reach their potential? That would be a proud legacy.

Like many of the ironies of life, those who spend their time encouraging others end up with a life story that encourages them, too.

Be an encourager. Cheer them on!

ON A SWING OR ON FIRE?

It is difficult for leaders to trust, but that is the only way to create both a productive workplace and one where the morale is strong. People sense when they are not trusted, no matter how we try to reassure them. How much you trust them is where the wisdom comes in, not whether to trust them. Trust must be earned, but like many things in life, you have to prime the pump and take a chance.

There are two types of trust opportunities to consider. They are what I call "swing" issues and "fire" issues.

Consider what it is like as a parent. There are many activities in which children have risks. As they learn to crawl, stand, walk and run, we know that they will fall down or get a bump. They must go through the experience of learning to do these challenges as part of their human development. It is not helpful for parents to stop them from going through these stages. We know that if they are on a swing, sooner or later they will fall off. That is okay. We will help them get up again and hop back on the swing. Over time, they will become very good at it. It is something they will master. The risks are not high, but the experience is worthwhile.

In contrast, if you saw a child approach a fire and reach their hand out toward the flame, you would intervene. That would not be the time to conclude that they will learn from the experience. The potential injury and the consequences are too grave to let them decide whether or not to reach into the fire.

In the same way, we must help our team to take the necessary steps to develop as people who are competent at what they do. Trusting your team members to do more of what they should be doing is good management. Will they make mistakes? Absolutely. Those can be teachable moments where we can review what happened, ask what they learned and give them some additional perspective for the next time. If they are going to do something that they are not prepared to do and where there are major negative consequences, those are the times when as leaders we must intervene. That is a way to not only protect the organization but them as well. This is part of a commitment to their success. If we expect their loyalty, team members must be certain that we are loyal to them too.

It is not unlike contrasting parenting styles. Two major factors in predicting the future well-being of children are support and management by their parents. Support is defined as knowing that you are loved and valued. Management is where you know what behaviors and choices are acceptable for yourself and in your relationship to others.

Draw a simple X and Y axis. Put the word "Support" on the vertical Y axis and "Management" on the horizontal X. That gives you four quadrants. (See Postscript chapter for more on this exercise.)

The bottom left area is where there is low support and low management. Write over that area neglected. The child does not have a firm sense that they are loved and the parent has not given them the necessary guidance to manage their behaviors.

The top left is the area representing high support and low management. Write over that area the term permissive. This parenting style affirms the love and value of the child but does not provide any boundaries.

The bottom right area has high management and low support. Write over that quadrant the term authoritarian. Here the parent manages the child's behavior but there is little or no sense of being loved and valued.

The top right area is where there is high support and high management. Label this area authoritative. The child knows deeply that they are loved and valued. They also learn the boundaries of behavior that will not cause harm but will serve others well.

As you might guess, the authoritative model is the most effective one. What might surprise you is that it is not the neglected model that is worst for children; it is the authoritarian approach. Rules without love are worse than no rules and no love.

While leaders do not play a parenting role and our team members are not our children, there are some transferable concepts here when it comes to providing environments of support and management. For employees, this might be translated as knowing "My leaders value me and want me to succeed. They also give me the clear and consistent expectations so that I can do it."

This reminds us that it is not only *where* we lead but *how* we lead our team.

Leaders should not be afraid to state their expectations. Activities must be measured and results must be quantified. That is consistent with high expectations for effectiveness and success. The other ingredient is also vital. Team members need to be trusted, valued and supported so that they can succeed too. That support needs to be affirmed just as often and just as clearly as the expectations for performance.

High support includes recognition. That can be done personally as a leader makes a comment face to face, sends an email or a note. It can also be corporate where the organization recognizes those who have done well. Heartfelt recognition is a great motivator for team members who are working hard.

Trust them as far as you can. Increase that trust by assigning more challenging roles where they have been trained to succeed. Limit their activities in areas where the risks are too great. Ask yourself: Are they on a swing or near a fire?

PLAYING A FRIENDLY

Have you ever thought about creating a success just for the sake of being successful? That may sound like either an exercise in vanity or futility, but it can actually be worthwhile for you and your group. Let's call it "playing a friendly" as they do in soccer.

In addition to the regular competitions of a soccer league and whatever special tournaments or international competitions are played, there are also "friendly matches" on the schedule.

These games are often mismatches in the sense that they are between two teams that may or may not be of a similar caliber. When a mismatch happens in a friendly, the underdog team benefits from playing a higher-ranked team with the possibility of raising their game through the increased competition.

One of the reasons a better team might play a lesser team is not just the idea of being sporting, but as a way to create success. The success may just be the win they achieve. It may also be the opportunity to fine-tune their system or combinations of players without the consequences of losing a match where the results count.

Sometimes it is helpful for the leader to create opportunities that are equivalent to playing a friendly match. These can be projects or activities where there is a high likelihood of success with a low risk of failure. The desired result is for the team to have the experience working together well and achieving a success. As with sports, you want to not only know what it is to win, but you want to experience what it feels like so that you can repeat it.

Additionally, you can use these friendly projects as a way to test out people in different roles or with added responsibilities. This can help to evaluate whether they are ready for a change in their position.

The other side of playing a friendly can also apply. You may want the team to experience a much larger challenge than they normally would to see how they respond to the added stresses. By limiting the downside in such an exercise, leaders can feel free to allow the team to play out the scenario as an evaluation tool. Militaries do this regularly in the form of "war games" to experience the battlefield without the full risk of facing an enemy who might actually want to hurt you or your team.

This can be helpful for leaders, as well. Sometimes you are in a project that is a prolonged exercise with little positive feedback available. For some types of leaders, this is just fine. Other leaders need the feedback to be more regular to validate the sacrifices being made for the team and the company. Look for a situation in which you can create success for yourself.

Remember, a "friendly" for a soccer team involves playing soccer, not baseball. That might seem obvious, but in creating a friendly game for your team to experience, you want to do something that relates to what the team normally does, not something completely different. For a team experience, design opportunities where people can learn, grow, and develop naturally. Give them the opportunity to succeed.

Following the success, use the experience to provide a time for reflection. What did the success feel like? Why did we succeed? Who contributed to the success? What went well? What are the things that you did well that you want to repeat and you want to do over again? What are the things that did not go so well that you want to be able to minimize next time or do differently? The process of reflection includes celebration and lessons learned to apply to a future experience where the consequences will be greater. That is all part of the learning process.

So as you look ahead in your schedule, do not be afraid to schedule a friendly game, too.

CHECK, PLEASE!

One of the great people I have met along the way is Dr. Bryce Taylor, MD. Dr. Taylor is Surgeon-in-Chief and Director of Surgical Services at the University Health Network and is a professor and associate chair in the Department of Surgery at the University of Toronto. He is also the author of the excellent book *Effective Medical Leadership*, published by Rotman-UTP Publishing. (He was also a star quarterback in his university days!)

As the chief of surgery for the University Health Network, Dr. Taylor oversees surgical teams who perform over 25,000 procedures a year in three hospitals.

I first met Dr. Taylor in the mid-1990s. He was an early adopter of IBM's ViaVoice speech recognition software, which he integrated into his dictation. Together we watched the progress of the software until it became a very useful product that would handle dictation at a rate of about 120 words per minute. It handled the many complex terms of medicine very well and recognized his voice with a high degree of accuracy.

Here was a surgeon, teacher and administrator who could have easily continued to do what had always been done in hospital dictation. Instead, he used the opportunity to enhance the productivity of his work. As great leaders tend to do, he wanted to find a better way.

In 2009, Dr. Taylor led the Canadian test of the Harvard/World Health Organization pilot project organized at eight hospitals around the world. The study was to test The Surgical Patient Safety Checklist as an innovation to reduce adverse events in surgery. The checklist was used at three critical points in the surgery: prior to anesthesia, immediately prior to incision, and finally prior to the patient leaving the operating room, the checklist was read aloud. All of the key elements of each step were reviewed to ensure that procedures were being followed exactly and that communication was clear.

Dr. Taylor and his team customized the template, and it is now used for all surgeries throughout their hospital network. The result has been a significant drop in the death rate and complications from surgery.

The insight that helped the surgeons to adopt the added steps in surgery was the use of a helpful analogy. The surgeons were reminded of the checklist used by pilots before takeoff. That checklist reduces errors that if found during takeoff, in the air, or at landing could be catastrophic. The review is not demeaning to the pilot. Instead, it is a recognition of the risks and a statement of the importance of the safety of passengers and crew.

That broke down any resistance, since they all recognized what brings value and importance to a plane full of people applies also to the one patient facing surgery.

This illustrates a tool for effective leaders. While the temptation is to continue to do what we have always done well, it is a good thing to cross-pollinate from other disciplines and even other industries or types of organizations. The tendency is to concentrate on those organizations that are most like us rather than those who might have a different pattern that might help us as well.

Leaders benefit from the generalist as well as the specialist. Many organizations tend to hire only specialists who are technically proficient in their area. To some degree, all leaders need to be able to be a generalist even if they began as a specialist with the organization. The ability to step back and see the bigger picture is part of the leader's role. Inventions often happen not just from a specialized approach to a problem but from the use of seemingly unrelated ideas to come up with a better solution. Many companies prize their generalists for problem solving as well as for long-term planning because they understand the interplay of past, present and future along with a wider worldview than many specialists require to do their work well.

If you are a generalist by nature or experience, you understand this. (Usually, you also have great admiration for those who can concentrate their talents and energies with such focus on an area.) If you are not a generalist, be sure that you have included them in your team. They might just come up with the next great idea borrowed from somewhere else that will give your organization the edge it needs.

It is great to think that it is not only at a restaurant that you hear the words "Check, please!"

THE POWER TO FORGIVE

It might surprise you to learn that forgiveness is one of the most popular topics I present at my seminars. It tends to be the one where more people come up to me and say how helpful it was for them. Sometimes it is long after the seminar that I receive a note saying how important it was in changing their life.

This is a brief synopsis of the big ideas covered at length in my presentations.

The power to forgive is a great gift we have all been given but seldom use. Many do not realize that they have this essential ingredient for keeping our relationships healthy.

The damage to relationships caused by the stresses and strains of life combined with our many careless moments leaves us all with many scars. From our most casual encounters to our most intimate relationships, we find many ways to let down and hurt those we hardly know, those we love dearly and those who are somewhere in between. This means we all have large and small offenses, both real and imagined, that consume our thoughts and emotions. Friends, family members, spouses, employers, colleagues, neighbors and strangers can offend us at any moment. Sooner or later (usually sooner!), someone will cross our boundary.

Even those of us not gifted in math have an amazing ability to calculate and file all of these offenses committed against us. We will even count those actions that were not done that we think should have been. Sins of commission and omission are all fair game. Like a high-speed computer, we can access these files at a moment's notice with all the gory detail included like a paparazzi account, where nothing is left out. As soon as we hear the person's name or see their face, it is all right there. Our muscles tighten and our fists clench at the thought of those who have wronged us again and again. Before long, we start to resemble the bitter old people we used to notice with curiosity as children.

The good news is that bitterness is not inevitable. There is a cure for our anger and hurt. The answer is in the power to forgive, something that we all have been given. It is the power to be free from the chains of painful and damaged relationships.

One of the common misconceptions when we talk about forgiveness is that it is better not to forgive: "That person does not deserve to be forgiven" or "What they did to me was so painful or hurts so much that I don't want to forgive them. I refuse."

That misses the point of the gift we have received with forgiveness. Forgiveness is primarily for the benefit of the person doing the forgiving. Yes, there are certainly some benefits for someone who has been forgiven, and that is important, too. But the first and principal benefit comes to the person who is willing to forgive. That's why we call it the power to forgive: When you choose to forgive, you are actually exercising your power in that relationship to move it forward and to take away the chains that very quickly surround a broken relationship.

Now to be clear, forgiveness is not the same as justice. So we are not talking here about crimes. This is not about something in the workplace that's inappropriate, illegal or against company policy. Those justice or legal issues have to be dealt with appropriately through the proper authorities. This is not hiding the facts about something that is going on that is wrong or illegal. I am not talking about that at all. Those offenses have to be dealt with appropriately. If a crime was committed, the authorities need to be notified. If it is something that violates company policy, that needs to be dealt with through the proper human resources channel or other authorities. Forgiveness is about how we process our feelings on the personal side.

As I work with people in conflict, I often discover that the person who hurt us often does not remember, never knew, or does not care about all the churning and turmoil created in your life. Now that is going to happen for a number of reasons. It could be because they did not intend to do anything or did not plan on doing anything to hurt the other person. Perhaps it was neglect, or maybe it was a lack of sensitivity. Often they do not have any memory of it because it wasn't something that never appeared on their radar.

For the person who has accumulated this long list of grievances, it may come as a great shock. They have spent their whole time going over and over this person's faults. The injured party who did nothing to offend them is bitter and upset. Yet the person who has offended them may not even remember the vexing experience.

All that energy is being spent on someone who was ignorant of the offense or who does not care to have a positive relationship with us. The potential joy and good of that relationship is lost over something they never knew. That is a tragedy.

Of course, there are things that are very legitimate where a person did something to undermine our relationship to hurt us. They might have worked to sabotage something in our life or to do something that was very terrible. I am not minimizing those kinds of actions, as they can be very real. Even with the most intentional hurts by someone against us, it is still in our best interest to forgive that other person. Without forgiveness, that person will always have a negative link to us.

We cut that negative connection by saying, "I am choosing to forgive that person." It does not deny your pain or claim that what happened did not happen. It does not assume that they deserved forgiveness, asked to be forgiven, or are even available to ask as they moved away or even died. It begins by making a decision—not because you feel like doing it. You choose to forgive to set yourself free.

BREAKING THE ICE

If someone has offended you, it might be helpful to share that with them. This of course depends on the nature of the relationship. Someone you will never expect to see again is probably not a good candidate to meet. However, if it is a colleague, family member or friend, it might be worth the effort to let them know how you are feeling. Done well and taken well, it can strengthen a relationship and avoid further conflict arising from careless behavior.

This should not be done as an ambush. It is best if it can be done in a neutral setting like a coffee shop that is casual over a cup of coffee or iced tea. The point of going beyond your choice to forgive is to rebuild the relationship. This needs to be shared carefully and with a humble approach. Ask if they would be willing to meet to discuss something that has been bothering you that you want to put behind you.

If you have that kind of relationship where they are willing to meet, think about what and how you are going to share your feelings. You might say, "I don't know if you are aware of this, but the other day at the office when you said this (or you did that), it really hurt me. I really felt awful about that, and it's been bothering me. I just wanted to talk to you to see if we can work that out."

Hopefully that other person's going to say, "Wow, I had no idea. I didn't know this was something between us to talk about, sort out or apologize for. Will you forgive me?" Then you can move on with that relationship. That's really the idea if that's possible.

It doesn't always work that way, though. Sometimes the other person is not available and willing to do that. They may wonder what all the fuss is about and just say that they did nothing wrong. Remember, you can still choose to forgive that person even if they do not ask to be forgiven or are unwilling to meet.

The next time you are reminded of what they did to offend you, practice forgiveness. Say, "Yes, I choose to forgive that person." Maybe you will see them across the table or at a meeting. Say to yourself, "I choose to forgive." By that practice you choose to move on, and that is very liberating. So one of the things that we encourage you to do is just to get into that practice of forgiving.

Do not be surprised if they use the occasion to bring up something that may have been bothering them about you. Do not interpret that as getting even. It is probably a sense that since we are dealing with uncomfortable topics, let me get this out of the way, too. Be prepared to ask for their forgiveness. Remember, like them, you may not have intended offense or even remember it, either. A humble attitude is required for the sake of moving the relationship back on track.

Just as we receive our fair share of offenses, even the most careful people will offend their co-workers, friends and family. You can always own up to your mistakes or missed opportunities by going to the person as soon as possible and acknowledging what happened. You will find most people are surprised that you would take the risk of doing that. They will respect the fact that you can not only recognize your mistakes but admit them, too. That is a powerful example for a leader to set.

So many people lose their energy, robbed of their vitality and their sense of the joy of life by these bitter feelings.

Even beyond forgiving, it is possible to forget, as well. That may sound impossible and you may be tempted to say, "I will forgive, but I won't forget!" That also keeps you from the more complete experience of moving past those things that hold us back.

If you get into the habit and practice of choosing to forgive, you will be surprised to find out that you really can also forget, as well. That gives you the freedom to move on to become your best self.

Who is Holding the Stakes?

Who are the stakeholders in your organization?

The concept of stakeholders includes those who have a stake in the effectiveness of an organization, government or company. One of the central roles of the board of directors of any organization is to protect and balance the interests of the many groups of stakeholders.

We tend to think of company owners as shareholders, but of course they are stakeholders too. The employees are included. Customers or clients who rely on the product or service certainly are as well. A broader definition that most people now include expands stakeholders to the larger community too. Some also include more nebulous entities such as the environment and nature, given the effect that some companies or governments can have on the wider world.

A leader may or may not deal directly with the wider interests of the stakeholders, depending on the responsibilities he or she has been given. Effective leaders are always aware of who the stakeholders are for their organization and how their decisions may impact the interests of these groups.

In the most basic sense, leaders serve the best interests of all involved. That is not an easy assignment.

That begins with serving those who are their leaders to the best of their ability. Leaders look for ways to be effective in carrying out the mandate they have been given to make their leaders succeed. In the same way, the leader works to make each of those on their team a success by building them up, supporting them and developing them in their roles on the team. Providing an excellent service or product is part of a leader's commitment to serving the clients and customers well.

As a leader, look for ways to also have an impact on your community as well. While many companies concentrate only on enriching their executives and shareholders, many companies have come to recognize community as an investment too. The reputation of a company as a good or bad corporate citizen does affect their brand and eventually their customer loyalty, including sales.

It is tempting for governments to lose sight of the full list of their stakeholders. While the public good and the environment might be easier for them to recognize, too often governments ignore the taxpayers as one of their stakeholder groups. They are more likely to look at voters as the important constituency to nurture. Not all taxpayers vote, and not all voters pay taxes. As governments are in the business of spending tax dollars they did not earn, it is always a risk that they will not be as careful with that money as they would be in spending their own. When a tax dollar has been collected, it has been entrusted to government to be spent well or not at all. The many important functions of government are undermined when government does not take seriously its role as a steward of the taxpayer's dollar.

Community organizations also spend someone else's money. Their stewardship of the grants and donations made in trust for the cause they serve is no less important. Leaders of community groups are accountable to those who fund the group. If those funds are not managed well, it is not just the donors who will be poorly served. Those who receive the services of the organization will eventually have fewer resources available when donations dry up.

Post-secondary educators have a special responsibility to the stakeholders we call students. These students are not only customers—they are also the future of our country. If they are not served with affordable, well-taught and well-run institutions, we undercut the competitive advantage of our country. We undermine the potential of the role that these students might play in our society. That robs our community of the well-educated and well-adjusted graduates who can contribute to a better tomorrow for all of us.

It was easier to just think of shareholders as the group we must satisfy. *Stakeholders* is a much more useful concept for leaders to embrace as we try to make a difference.

Who are your stakeholders? What have you done for them lately?

TELL ME A STORY

If you asked leaders how many of the myriad memos they remember from the thousands that pass through their email and over their desk, the answer (including the eloquent groan) is very few. Ask them about a good anecdote they heard at work, on the other hand, and most will light up to regale you with a great tale.

We remember stories. We learn from stories. That is why great leaders are also great storytellers.

As part of your leadership, learn how to pick and share a good story. This will help those serving with you to connect better to the big idea that you wish them to learn and remember.

There are many reasons that stories engage us differently than a memo of facts. Facts tend to engage the left side of the brain only. We sort and file these bits of information into a place where hope we can retrace our "brain-steps" if we ever need them again. In a story, we create many different connections to the listener as we engage not just the analytical left side of the brain but also the creative right side. Our use of images, different vocabulary, drama, suspense, humor and whatever else might be in the story (and the way we tell it!) engages the emotions, as well. The listener has the opportunity to emotionally engage with the facts of the story as well as the surrounding scene. Some of the emotions may be positive. Others may be negative, depending on the subject matter. The story might even touch on some nobler themes that appeal to our sense of fairness, compassion, duty, honor and so much more. A person's value system may even be engaged by what they hear.

What a good story does do is create what marketers call "stickiness." Stickiness describes that you are more likely to remember and connect to that information and the experience shared with you. Leaders want what they share to have that same "stickiness" since that will increase the potential of those we serve to be able to carry out and transfer the ideas that have been shared.

Most cultures were built on storytelling through stories, songs, poetry, drama and art. This was not just a way to pass the time but a way to pass on our life. Stories were told of dangers to be avoided. Some dramas told of heroism to be admired. Ideas about a way of life were illustrated. How to perform tasks that were essential for survival were shared and rehearsed. Even profound questions about the universe and the meaning of life often were reflected in the stories of ancient cultures.

For most of our history, it was the oral tradition that was more important than that which was written. Your word was what mattered. The great storytellers of any generation and all cultures were celebrated as much as the warriors. Indeed, it was the "hi-stori-ans" who shaped how the warrior's deeds would be remembered. Whether you were the priest, troubadour, bard, balladeer or vaudevillian, your recounting of the stories of the culture mattered.

In our time, those who create the novels, newspapers, magazines and histories are joined by the many other ways that stories are told today through film, ballet, music, television, video games and more.

If stories matter, how do you as a leader tell a good story?

Some people are natural storytellers. Others never thought of themselves as such and so never try. For those of us who have had the benefit of great storytellers in our family, we understand how a good tale can enrich not just the moment but our relationships, as well.

Stories, like jokes, usually have a form to them. (All those lessons from your early elementary and secondary literature classes really were important!)

Think of knock-knock jokes. "Knock-knock." "Who's there?" "Cash." "Cash-who?" "No thanks, but I will have a peanut."

They have a very specific formula that is followed. Speaker: "Knock-knock." Responder: "Who's there?" Speaker: "(Something)" Responder: "(Something)-who?" Speaker: Then the punch line that usually is a pun or a play on the sound of the combined words.

The form of most stories usually begins with an introduction of the characters, place and scene. Then there is the event, dilemma or crisis. Finally, there is a resolution. If it is a humorous story, the ending involves a surprise or something unexpected. Depending on the idea you are illustrating, you might have a conclusion that connects the story to what you want the team to know. A great story makes that so obvious, the connection often does not need to be said.

Start looking for the skeleton of stories you hear told in your world and in entertainment. You will begin to detect these kinds of patterns.

Not every idea needs a story attached to it. If the challenge is urgent, you may have no time for a story. Watch the reaction of your listeners to see if they are engaged or bored. Keep stories brief. But if you wish to have an idea that sticks, try what has worked down through history in all cultures.

Tell them a story.

STAGE COACH

No matter who you are, there are some common stages of personal development that we will all experience. It is worthwhile to learn about these stages since sooner or later, you too will be there. It is also helpful for you to take advantage of the characteristics of that stage and to minimize the risks that come with each of the stages.

Part of my background is in psychology studies. The focus was the area of developmental psychology. There are many branches of psychology, but I believe this one is particularly useful for most people. Simply stated, developmental psychology is focused on observation. Psychologists do long-term studies where they observe how people develop and change over many years. Through these observations, they detect patterns that are similar and common for most people. People go through the stages at different speeds, but everyone goes through them all as part of a normal life.

A developmental approach allows people to develop through these stages at their own pace. And that is okay. There is "work" to be done through each of the stages of personal development. How well we do that work will influence how strong we will be when we come through that stage and enter the next.

One of the reasons that I prefer the developmental psychology approach compared to some of the other branches is that it is based on observation – how we as humans really are.

I would recommend that you do some reading on each of these developmental psychologists and sociologists, such as Jean Piaget, Virginia Satir, Eric Ericson and Lawrence Kohlberg, to name just a few. You can find some excellent summary articles on the web.

Here I will highlight one of the people who have studied something that leaders will have to face personally as well for individuals on their team.

You may be familiar with the stages of grief described by Elisabeth Kübler-Ross in the late '60s, in which she defined the grieving process. People who have lost someone to death or some other catastrophic loss can expect to go through the stages of denial and isolation, then anger, followed by bargaining, then depression and finally acceptance.

Leaders will have to deal with people who are facing loss in their lives outside of the workplace. It can happen over time, as with the slow passing of a parent. It might be a sudden loss of a loved one or friend in an accident. A divorce or loss of employment is also a shock for many people, who then have to "grieve" the changes that this will create in their lives. The death of a spouse or a child is one of the most painful experiences to endure.

Some corporate human resources or employee relations departments offer support services for those going through a difficult time. If your group does not have that, it is helpful to encourage the person to seek out support in their community or faith organizations, counseling or friends as needed.

While executives cannot become counselors for their team, effective leaders understand how to show empathy and support for those going through life's many challenges. Being available to meet with the team member to acknowledge or recognize the loss is helpful. At times, the person may want to know you care when you ask how they are doing. Asking the same question on another day may trigger a curt or negative response. Do not take these changes personally, as the person will experience many waves in the grief process that may want expression or privacy.

Knowing the process of grieving will help the leader to be sensitive to the ups and downs that the team member will experience as all humans normally will. There may be times when the person will seem perfectly fine. Other times, they may seem distracted or depressed as they get used to the loss they have experienced. A leader needs to flex with this wherever possible.

Human relationships are always changing from levels of celebration to levels of grief, with some flat periods in between. It is great when we can, as was said long ago, "Rejoice with those who rejoice and weep with those who weep." Leaders who do this show care for the person as well as completion of the task. That earns loyalty and respect that pays off with a more effective team in the long run.

Knowing the process of grieving will help the leader to be sensitive to the ups and downs that the team member will experience as all humans normally will. There may be times when the person will seem perfectly fine. Other times, they may seem distracted or depressed as they get used to the loss they have experienced. A leader needs to flex with this wherever possible.

Human relationships are always changing from levels of celebration to levels of grief, with some flat periods in between. It is great when we can, as was said long ago, "Rejoice with those who rejoice and weep with those who weep." Leaders who do this show care for the person as well as completion of the task. That earns loyalty and respect that pays off with a more effective team in the long run.

MAGIC WANDS AND MAGIC LAMPS

Sooner or later, all leaders wish that they had something enchanted available to use. Leaders run into some challenges that seem to defy their thinking and best efforts. Try as they might, nothing seems to work.

If only they could pull out a magic wand. One or more waves of the stick and some suitable phrases could manage the intractable difficulties. (Sometimes they might imagine making certain people disappear to a faraway place without the Internet. But I digress…)

If, on the other hand, one could find a magic lamp, that would have its advantages, too. The clever CEO would know that they had three wishes for the magic lamp. They would wish for three more as the first wish before using the next couple of wishes to solve the top two problems on the agenda. (It would be up to accounting to keep track of the unused wishes as a part of a magical line of credit.)

Of course, most people do not have an ample supply of wands (Where was Ollivander's store again?), and the magic lamps seem to be reserved for the movies. As the books and movies also show, people rarely make the right wishes, never foreseeing the unintended consequences.

However, what we do have is something that can be just as enchanted and perhaps more practical. There are people in our life who can serve as wise advisers. Think about King Arthur and the Arthurian legends. One of the most reassuring characters in those stories was the wizard Merlin. He was there to guide and give sage (wise) advice to the king. Kings and queens need sages, the wise women and men who were there with them. Harry Potter et al. benefited from the guidance of Headmaster Dumbledore in J. K. Rowling's tales.

I particularly love the J. R. R. Tolkien stories *The Lord of the Rings* and *The Hobbit*. In those stories you have the character Gandalf, who was there as the wandering wizard who was able to come alongside a king or a leader and give wise counsel. Sometimes the counsel of Gandalf the Grey was tempered with uncertainty, but its wisdom lay in choosing the ways that would lead to the most honest end.

The same is true in our leadership today. Who are the wise people around you? Their wisdom could be from years of experience as a leader. Perhaps they may be someone who is wise because of their intuitive sense about working with others. Some are gifted in their business intelligence and are able to perceive opportunities to take and dangers to avoid.

Finding trusted advisers should be a priority for every leader. Some companies have assembled a talented board of directors who can provide feedback and guidance to the CEO as needed. Community groups often have well-informed boards of advisors who will share insights with the leadership.

Presidents of the United States and leaders in other countries often have a set of advisors who are different from those appointed to the official posts of cabinet secretary. Often they come with them on their political journey from their home states. Ronald Reagan had his "California kitchen cabinet" of old friends and advisors. Jimmy Carter had his crew from Georgia, and George W. Bush included his Texans. Barack Obama included many advisors from Chicago.

These key relationships have a special trust and working knowledge of the leader built over time and in challenging experiences. They are also seen as having no personal agenda to promote beyond helping the leader be successful with the heavy responsibilities that they must meet every day.

As with most leadership models, while you may not be able to afford to bring your best and trusted friends with you to work every day, find one or two people who fit the qualifications of a wise person to be there for you.

More valuable to a leader than just a confidant is a mentor. Do not assume that having a mentor means that you are any less of a leader or that somehow you are not ready for the responsibility. Mentors play a very large role in our personal and professional development. Often leaders have mentors who guide them at work and then older friends who mentor them in the everyday aspects of life outside of work. Sitting down for that monthly coffee or having that phone chat can give you perspective and grace that comes from being with wise people.

You may have to be proactive in the workplace to find a mentor. While many companies recognize its value, most do not have a formal process to ensure that it happens. Find more senior people in your organization who can not only guide you in a crisis but who can help you develop as a leader.

What you can or should share with such a confidant depends on the nature of your business. You may have fiduciary or privacy issues that limit the kinds of details that you can discuss with someone outside the company. Even within the company, you may have to exercise discretion in what you can appropriately discuss. A wise counselor will resist hearing details or topics that they sense are beyond the scope that they should have, as well.

For many people and companies today, the choice is an executive coach. They are skilled to help you sort through not only the process of the leadership challenges but will have that role of a supportive friend who is working for your success. As someone mandated by the company, they can serve a confidential role, if that is what the leader and the company decide.

So if you happen to see a wandering wizard in your travels, ask him or her to tea. You will be glad you did.

ROBES AND CROWNS

There are many symbols of leadership. Some spring from ancient traditions; others come from religious roots. Many are colorful. Others are purposely dark and unremarkable. It is helpful for leaders to understand what symbols to use and what will hinder your leadership.

In a very basic sense, these symbols are used to distinguish the leader from the rest of the team. In many corporations, you know the rank of the leader by what floor they occupy. How large is their office? Do they have a great view? Do they have the corner office?

In ancient times, a crown would identify a king or queen. Royal robes would be rich and colorful, announcing the high standing of the monarch. Religious leaders in some traditions wear very colorful vestments that include significant shades and hues that remind the onlookers of some of their religious beliefs. These clothes and other accoutrements announce the importance of the wearer.

In contrast, the judiciary in many countries wear very plain robes that are usually black. This is, in part, to announce the seriousness of the occasion but also to create a uniformity that would suggest that you would receive similar treatment before any of those who wear the same gown.

Combinations of gowns, hoods and hats distinguish levels of achievement among academics at formal occasions. The academic gown suggests that an undergraduate degree is completed. The addition of a hood tells you that a master's degree has been attained. A hat often indicates a doctorate received. Colors and styles often announce the school where the top degree was earned.

Rings tell us of a school attended or a marriage commitment. Rank on a soldier announces comparative seniority to others of a lower position. Medals symbolize meritorious service or achievement. Badges announce our right to be someplace where there are restrictions. Some uniforms, like a physician's scrubs, are more practical to allow them to better perform their tasks. A chain of office tells you that someone is a mayor.

The effect of most symbolic clothing for leaders is to elevate the person wearing the clothing outside of the ordinary. This is a reward for the person where achievement has been recognized as a leader, but it is also a cue to those who follow who the leader is. (This was especially valuable before Wikipedia became the standard of whether you were a sufficiently worthy individual to warrant a page by the Wiki powers that be. But I digress…)

An important purpose of these symbols is cover the person with the office. Like a robe, we are to see the symbol more than the person wearing it. We are to respect the office or position that the person holds. Even when we disagree with or even dislike the person, the civilized response is to respect the office she or he represents.

We may not like the judge's rulings, but we must show deference to the honor of the court. Otherwise we receive a contempt citation, rightly named because we have shown contempt for the judge as a part of the justice system. If we disagree with the ruling, we appeal the decision. If all of our appeals fail, we live with the decision as part of living in a society of laws. It is for that reason that when a judge betrays that trust, the consequences are severe, since it brings the system into disrepute.

Whether you are a leader with a name tag or someone who has other indications of rank and responsibility, it is vital that you remember the purpose of the trust that those symbols represent. Ultimately, they are all purposed for some form of service unless they are perverted by pride or power. We therefore have to be very careful not confuse ourselves with the power entrusted to our care for the benefit of those we serve. Nor should we use symbols to enhance ourselves at the expense of others.

As followers, we have to fight the waves of contempt that modern societies heap upon not just the individual leaders but also the institutions they serve. Those who complain are rarely willing to do what it takes to become a leader. If we are not very careful, the institutions that we criticize for their ineffectiveness stop playing a role in our society. We might not be prepared for that brave new world that is led by cults of personality without the continuity and the checks and balances that institutions place in providing peace, order and good government. When we have followed leaders who are only qualified by their personality, we have usually been disappointed or worse.

There are also alternative symbols that, through their simplicity, remind us of the call of leaders to serve. Some of the most profound leaders in history led not with a general's uniform or a king's crown but through the authenticity of an unremarkable nun's habit like Mother Theresa, the khandi worn by Gandhi, or the simple white robe of Jesus Christ.

Symbols matter. Recognize them. Respect them. Use them well to serve.

THE HUMAN CONDITION

What about your weaknesses? If you are the kind of person who can identify some weaknesses in your leadership, that is a huge advantage. Understanding that you are not perfect adds a dash of humility that always serves a leader well.

In the executive coaching process, we look at ways to identify your strengths, weaknesses and passions. Self-awareness helps us make better decisions since we have fewer blind spots than the person who just continues on as if there were no problems to consider. It also reduces the natural tendency to see every failure as someone else's fault. A leader sees the successes and the failures of her or his group as a team problem to be solved.

One of the most common failures of leaders is the lack of listening. Even those who are otherwise careful listeners often stop paying attention to what others are saying unless it is to hear what they wish to hear. That kind of insulation from what others might be trying to tell us damages our leadership and leads to "groupthink" where everyone believes they all agree when really they stopped asking the tough questions.

Take time to listen to what others are saying. Listening is not the same as agreeing. But it is better to hear what others are saying (and thinking) before decisions are made in case that information might change your course of action.

If you have a hard time really paying attention to what others are saying and hearing, there are some exercises that you can do. The "dyadic encounters" are good example of this, but there are many other exercises and processes that you can go through to start to learn how to be a better listener. You may not be as natural as somebody else at it, but you can learn to listen well. It is a skill to be learned and honed.

Whatever the weaknesses are, recognize that sometimes our weaknesses and vulnerabilities are part of what makes us effective. It is not just the strengths; it is also the weaknesses. That combination makes us human, and others will respect the fact that we "get it." Sometimes having a struggle makes us more natural and approachable. Our recognition of weaknesses is a healthy reminder that we need to rely on others to be successful rather than a self-made person who needs no one. Coming across as somebody who cares and has both strengths and weaknesses will be more effective.

Concentrating too much on your weaknesses and flaws will also undermine your leadership. You need to have self-confidence. Self-confidence does not mean you are deluded into thinking that you are self-made. It does mean that you can include all the benefits and skills you have received from family, friends, teachers and experiences over your lifetime to apply to your leadership. We are always building on who we are.

As a leader, you are always in the people business. If you are going to be effective in the people business, you have to pay attention to people. They continue to learn from you, and you should continue to interact with them and gain from their experiences. Continue to benefit from who they are.

Surround yourself with sharp and interesting people, not just at work but in your social and community life. That will be stimulating and will sharpen your communication skills. A broad life, like a liberal arts education, creates not only a more interesting person but a more flexible leader who can draw from a larger pool of experiences.

Your goal is not to control others but rather to be a positive influence in their lives to help them succeed. For that reason, you do not need to fear the competition from hiring the best and the brightest for your team. The best leaders lead great teams full of talented people who together succeed sooner than expected and under budget.

So the next time you are tempted to despair that "I am only human," use it as a reason to celebrate an ingredient of being a great leader!

3-D LEADERS

I believe that a vibrant spiritual life is essential to a balanced personal life. Just as when we do not feed our mind or have healthy emotional outlets we become weak, so too do we need to develop and feed the spiritual dimension of who we are.

Spirituality as discussed here includes a wide range of life experiences, from a simple awareness of nature to appreciating harmony and beauty in our world, listening to music, and taking time to reflect and meditate on life, or it can be through religious or faith experiences, as well. It touches those elements not just of how we exist in life but those things that add meaning.

This spiritual dimension reminds us of what is truly important in life. It has been said that if you seek happiness, you will never find it. Happiness is a by-product of making good choices and serving others. In the same way, you will be more successful in your business and life if you have the balance that feeding your spiritual life includes.

Get a life and keep that life! If you have family available, spend time with them. That is not just important for them; it is vital for you. There is nothing like a separation or divorce to damage your energy levels and career potential. Many relationships would survive and thrive if enough time were committed to them. The same is true with children. Missing the soccer games or school concerts will be remembered long after the "important" reason you were not there is forgotten.

Teams that recognize the value of the whole person and give time to feed the spirit, soul and body outside of work will be much more productive.

If you do not take time off on a regular basis, you will burn out. You will be less effective. Take time each day to pause and reflect. Walk around. Step outside. Do a stretch. All of these little decisions will change your sense of well-being.

On your days off, be off. Vacations are a necessity! Forget the thinking that says you do not have the time or you will miss that big sale. Take regular vacation breaks to recharge your battery.

One of the challenges I see in the life of most executives I meet is the need for time to decompress. That is not just being away from the office with your tablet glowing and your smartphone buzzing, beeping and flashing. It is not only good for you to be out of touch for a while—it is healthy for your office to learn to do without you. That is part of mentoring and is a recognition that you will not always be there. They need the experience of making it all work and solving problems as they arise.

Model that healthy approach to relationships to your team, as well. Try to avoid contacting them outside of work hours so they too can concentrate on their home life. Even waiting until morning to send your emails will take away the panic that some team members have that they might miss some critical instruction if they are not checking for messages. Remember, to you it might just be the convenience of sending a thought when it occurs. Diligent team members might take the casual timing on your part as a sign of urgency for them to respond or prepare for the next day's encounters.

Remember that when some leaders think they are whispering, team members hear shouting. Go the extra mile to encourage the team to invest time in their outside work life. You will have a more interesting and energized team at work.

Seminars, workshops and retreats are also invaluable tools for your personal development. Beyond the information they provide, going on these kinds of events allows you to step away from your everyday experiences to learn and have fellowship with others. It is especially helpful if it includes people from different walks of life where you can explore more than just your industry stats and market trends.

Be a 3-D leader. You will stand out in an otherwise flat world of 2-D leaders who have yet to discover the spiritual dimension of leadership.

EXIT STAGE RIGHT

There comes a point where we have to allow leaders to exit the stage. Leadership is a temporary condition, and every leader in any organization, group, or country sooner or later will be done. One of the tasks that is very difficult for leaders is to choose their time of departure. A mark of a wise leader is that they time their departure well.

We have all seen the people who cling to an office, entertainment role or sport well beyond the time when they could be effective. People wonder aloud that they seem to have no friends or family who care enough to tell them that it is time to leave the stage. Their earlier contributions are clouded by their lack of awareness or need to continue well beyond when they should have retired.

The prospect of ending a role is often conflicted. The idea of a fresh start in a new role or retirement may be appealing. The sense of unfinished business and unfulfilled dreams can compel us to continue on. There is a relief in the prospect of being done with the challenges and weight of leadership. But will the next role be vital enough for me, or was this the best it will ever be?

There certainly are some roles that are a zenith experience. When you leave the presidency of the United States after two terms, you cannot be reelected. You join the famous and very small club of ex-presidents. The end of that role is a big adjustment to make for any person. Some former presidents have found a meaningful life after office, while others seem to have never really recovered, haunted by what was not accomplished in their time as commander in chief.

Those who do well in transition usually have understood the difference between their job (what I am working at today) and their career (what my lifetime of work has been). The ability to separate the two actually gives you more freedom to work better at any job and create a more successful career. Like many things in life, things we hold onto desperately usually do not go well compared to those we embrace comfortably.

The other characteristic of people who resign or retire well is that they do not confuse their employment with their identity as a person. The business card may attach a title next to your name. People do ask what your position is in the company. All of that is not who you are; it is what you do. Is this the only place you could do what you do? Of course not. Is this the only thing you can do? That is probably not true, either. You are not your job, as great as you may be at doing it.

It is true that our work is very important. It is beneficial to work in ways that are far more important than the monetary reward. Being productive and making a difference with our time is a positive part of being human. That is why massive unemployment and especially youth unemployment is so dangerous to the long-term health of a country. It is also why unemployment for those older workers not yet at retirement age feeds depression and despair.

Some executives have a clear sense of objectives they wish to accomplish while they are the leader. Once those objectives are reached, they understand themselves well enough to say it is time to move on. Other people have a type of internal clock that only allows them to stay at a position for a certain number of years before they are ready for a change.

If it is not a straightforward retirement, leaders need to conduct regular assessments within themselves and through conversations with those they love and trust. Is this the time to stay or to go? Am I continuing to be effective here? Is there someone else in the organization ready to take over for me? Could they now do a better job than I could?

Swiss psychiatrist Paul Tournier noted that in life, people have to know whether it is time to resist or to surrender. Resistance is not a question of strength but of decision. Surrendering is not a sign of weakness but a decision to stop. It is a challenge for many people to know whether the time is right to stay or to go.

While it is a practical consideration to know what job you are going to have next, you may need to take a step into the grey fog of uncertainty. If it has come to the point that you no longer have the confidence that you should stay, it is probably time to start working on an exit strategy.

This is different from having opposition within or without toward your leadership. Leaders are often criticized for what they do or do not decide. If you are making the best decisions you can and believe that you are on the right course, stick with it. Do not let others force you out, but do not stay because others agree it is time you left and you do not want to appear pushed. Make your own decision regardless of support or opposition.

But there comes a point when leaders sense that the time has come. That can occur not when there is trouble, but when all is going very well. Like a good investment, you want to sell on a high note, not when your stock is down. Too many leaders are forced to leave on a bad note when a short time earlier, they could have finished a good run of leadership at a positive point.

Understanding the principles discussed earlier also helps with a transition. If we believe that our role as leaders is to be a good steward of the trust placed in us to serve our stakeholders, what is best for others is more important than what is best for us. Taking care of the best interests of those we serve is the only way to ensure that this job will not damage our career.

That is why it is helpful to have a succession plan in place from the start of your leadership. All of us are vulnerable to accident, illness or death. If we care about protecting the group we lead, we must ensure that there others who know what you know if it becomes necessary to transfer the operation and leadership of your group. Some leaders do not share power due to their insecurity as people. They believe that power is finite and a zero-sum game. If I share my knowledge with you, I will have less power. The opposite is true. A grasping and secretive attitude leads to huge knowledge gaps for others who might have to step in during a crisis. It is better to create a knowledge backup system so that a transition can be as smooth as possible if needed.

How long should your transition take? Once again, those you trust will have some guidance for you. Depending on the level of your position, your board may want a longer time to allow for a smoother transition. Other companies prefer that once you have decided to leave, you do so quickly.

Leaving suddenly can be a shock to your system. You will need some time to decompress after a change, but do not confuse refreshment with doing nothing. Find ways to be active in other areas of your life. Catch up on some extra family time. Finish some projects that have been waiting. Do some recreation. Staying busy and vital is important in a smooth transition for you. A sudden stop can give you emotional and spiritual whiplash.

If you are leaving over a longer time, beware of the danger of checking out mentally and emotionally. It is difficult to keep the same level of commitment and energy if you know that you are leaving. We go through some very normal processes of detachment in order for us to be able to be ready for when that job is no longer ours. However, we need to balance that with a higher commitment to finishing well for the sake of those we continue to serve.

Is it time to resist, or is it time to surrender? Either way, choose to serve the best interests of those who have trusted you as their leader.

IT'S BEEN AN HONOR

It is time for us to start honoring our leaders again. We live in a society that is highly skilled at tearing people down. Anyone who steps up to the plate and is willing to be a leader is often criticized even before he or she gets started. It has a chilling effect on many people who might otherwise be willing to serve as a leader.

The result is that we have leaders who either are so thick-skinned that they are insensitive to criticism or we have others who have an unhealthy compulsion to be in control. It makes it more difficult to recruit good people who look at the "attack dogs included" in serving and decide it is not worth their time.

Savage political attacks on leaders is nothing new. History is filled with them. However, the escalation and intensity enabled by social media means that being constantly under attack is much more pervasive. We live in a time when we need our best and our brightest to not just be on Wall Street but to also in politics, the judiciary and other areas of public service.

Leaders are not above criticism. Many times they deserve it. But followers seem to believe they are immune from criticism, as well. Society wants leaders to take away all the pain, the risks and the uncertainties of life at little or no cost. The public says, "Give me unlimited benefits, control spending and do it with little or no taxes required." When leaders do so to pacify the protests or to lock in votes for the next election, they are criticized for failing to lead.

Our leaders may have problems leading, but most of us have a very tough time following. It would be interesting to see leaders give their constituents an "approval rating" to reflect how well they are following. Would our scores be as dismal as the leaders often are? Leadership is always a partnership between leaders and followers. If leaders do not lead well or if followers choose not to follow, chaos will result.

The contempt for leaders carries over to institutions, as well. The effect is to undermine the structures of a civil society that allow individuals the freedoms that we value most. Free speech, the rule of law, respect for others and the principles of community are increasingly abandoned to a bygone era. Little wonder that so many who might otherwise be willing to serve the public choose to pursue other options.

Leaders here must also set their own example. How often do politicians and executives choose to begin their time at the helm by criticizing their predecessor? The last CEO or president becomes the reason for all the current problems. That mantra is continued until at least the next election and beyond if the public buys into the argument. We have seen how easy it is for candidates to criticize those in office and disparage their policies only to learn that once in power, they might have been right after all. That in itself is not a bad thing if the new leaders are able to say that they were wrong and now understand it better. Wait for it…

The tragedy is that we all lose when we do not have the best people leading us at all levels. The time has come to start honoring our leaders again. We do a better job at honoring our celebrities than we do those who serve our community.

Honoring our leaders does not require us to believe that they are perfect or that every decision they make is one that I would have made; that is just not going to happen. However, we can hopefully honor the many people who are serving out of a willingness to make a difference for others.

It is said that the ancient Biblical injunction to "Honor your mother and father" is as much for our benefit as for theirs. Not only does a grateful attitude help us sleep better—it creates a pattern in societies that practice it. If we model honoring our parents, there is a greater likelihood that our children might honor us, with all the failures and inadequacies that every parent has.

The same is true for leaders. If we practice a pattern that does not honor our leaders, we might find that when it comes our turn to lead, our leadership is not respected. Listen to candidates in elections tear down the incumbents who are leading in order to win the election who then are amazed that others will not show them the respect needed to lead effectively once they are the leader.

It is an honorable thing to be willing to serve others as a leader. We need to work on being better as followers so we can engage the best people to step forward for us to have a better tomorrow.

If leadership has come knocking at your door, open the door. You might be trembling and fearful. Grab those opportunities for leadership with the right attitude. Use your head, use your heart, and use your hope, and you will make a difference not only in the group you lead, but also in your world.

DEVELOPING OLD FRIENDS

One of the greatest titles we can have is "old friend." We never appreciate how important old friends are until we are older. The problem is that we need to start our old friendships when we are young. We then have to nurture and grow those friendships over our middle age, when a busy life and changing geographies can cause us to neglect those friends.

Leaders especially need to have old friends.

With the challenges of leadership, you often find that you cannot socialize in the same way that you could before you had the executive position. Many celebrities and wealthy people wonder aloud whether the new relationships they make are there because of who they are as people or because of their fame and wealth. It often haunts them and destroys their current relationships, if not addressed. In contrast, they will speak fondly of those relationships that stretch back before they had their success or money. Those friendships were the ones that they knew were authentic since they did not have other motivations to cloud the relationship.

Another feature of old friendships is that they understand more of your history. They have been in your story for a long time and may have walked with you through the mountaintop experiences as well as the dark valleys that are included in your tale. Hopefully you have been there for them through their ups and downs, too. The fact that they still accept you is valuable.

The fact that leaders make the time to invest in relationships outside of the workplace is also important. If work is all-consuming to the point that we do not have time for friendships, it is likely that we are undermining our leadership abilities. Without the refreshment and interaction that genuine friendships provide, people tend to lose some of the common touch that authentic relationships bring.

This is especially true if you are in a leadership position where people tend to be deferential to you. It is easy to begin to see your relationships from a layered perspective. You perhaps have seen the great cartoon where the boss is introducing an employee to someone by saying, "May I introduce you to my immediate inferior, Bill Smith?" It is easy in those environments to confuse someone's respect and deference to your position with you being a superior person.

Friendships, by their very nature, are about equality. You may have varying degrees of intimacy with a friend from an acquaintance to a close friend to a best friend, but they are all based on being friends. Friends are not superior or inferior.

Spending time with friends, and especially old friends, brings us back to the reality that we are who we once were. We have added new experiences and perhaps resources to the story. That in itself does not really matter between friends.

Keeping old friends does take work, often during the most busy times of life when careers and other obligations are at their peak. Leaders especially need to make time to be with their friends. The temptation is to assume that you can wait until things are not so busy. Then you will catch up. Perhaps those friends will be there for you then. Maybe they will be gone. What you will have lost (and they will have lost as well) is the benefits of friendship during times of your life when it might be the most helpful. Friendship is a great antidote to the arrogance of power because friends will not tolerate it.

If you have not continued to be in touch with your friends, restarting those relationships may be awkward at first. It may be uncomfortable for someone from the old neighborhood to connect with you in a different stratum of economic life. You need to be sensitive to that in making your connections. Some people will be reluctant to connect again for fear that they could not afford the restaurants where you might go. Visiting your home might make them self-conscious if they feel that you would be uncomfortable in their home.

Some people handle another's generosity comfortably on the basis that if the roles were reversed, they too would do the same. Others find it difficult because they feel that they have not achieved what you have. Like all friendships, these are things you have to sense with each other and find what is comfortable and what works. That will take some care and sensitivity as well as a commitment to keeping the friendship alive and well.

So if you have not been in touch with some old or current friends for a while, pick up the phone, open Skype or send an email. Keep those connections alive and well.

Perhaps the greatest rewards in friendship come in the later years of life. When the intensity of leadership and work mellows with age, your life passages concentrate more and more on relationships. You are more aware of the importance of your children, grandchildren and siblings. You begin to understand in a deeper way that it is not what we do or what we have that makes us who we are. Old friends are people who understand that and us best at that stage of life.

You are making investments in your retirement saving accounts for a golden retirement. Be sure to make investments each and every year in your friendship accounts, as well. That may be the most valuable part of your portfolio when you are retired.

Who would you like to have as an old friend when you are retired? Today is the day to invest in those people we hope will call us "old friend" in the years to come.

SAIL ON

If you have read this book, it probably means that you are already in a leadership experience. Some are reading this in the hopes of being a leader. Others have a sneaking suspicion that it might be their turn soon.

I hope that the message you have heard here is that being a leader is a very good thing. It is often not an easy thing, but it will be very rewarding as an experience in your life.

Those who have found life worthwhile often find their meaning in serving others. That service can be as a leader or a follower. It can be part of something large or just brightening the corner where you are. Either way, having an attitude that recognizes the value in helping others will bring you rewards far beyond anything you could receive in your bank account.

If you are someone who wants to be a leader, get busy now doing whatever you have to do make others successful where you are. When you create a pattern that puts others first, people notice. The little responsibilities that you handle well create opportunities for something more important later. As the Bible aptly says, "He who is faithful in little will be faithful in much." Start leading where you are with the chances you are given.

The other big idea that I hope you catch from this book is the idea of being a positive influence in your leadership rather than someone who is in control. All leaders need to multiply themselves through the team around them. None of us can do it all. Someone who is a positive influence will encourage others to reach their potential. That enlarged and strengthened team pulling together will achieve so much more than a team that is resisting a tyrant.

Leadership has risks. Leaders will fail as well as succeed. Remember that if your energies are to make others successful in reaching their potential, there is nothing to regret however the short-term results may appear.

Be sure to use your head, your heart and your hope as a leader. Your team will benefit from that kind of whole-person approach to leadership.

Do not be afraid to ask for help when needed. Go to the resources in your group like a senior manager to help you in a tough time. Reach out to your human resources professionals for support. Engage your trusted friends and mentors to give you the sage advice you need at a critical time. If you need help, go early. Most problems only get worse over time. Many can be corrected quickly if they are caught early. There is no shame in asking for help. There is no excuse for putting your team at risk because you were afraid to be embarrassed.

I hope that you will have the opportunity to engage an executive coach sometime. Even if it is for a limited time, you will find insights and perspectives that can feed your career for a long time to come.

Finally, I would be glad to hear from you. Send your feedback about the book or your own leadership experiences – the good the bad and the ugly. Leaders appreciate what other leaders are going through.

So if you are a leader – lead! If you are not yet a leader – follow and be prepared to lead when it is your turn.

Hop aboard and sail on to worlds unknown. It will give you a great story to tell the grandkids someday.

THE EXECUTIVE COACH

What is executive coaching?

My goal is a simple one: Develop effective, sustainable and renewable leaders.

To be effective as a leader, we believe that a person has to be able to apply what is needed when it is needed to the opportunity they have to be the leader.

Sustainable leadership means that a person is not a flash in the pan or someone who is only able to lead for a short term before their effectiveness fades. Instead, with a whole-person focus, they will understand how to not just sprint but do the leadership marathon, as well.

Renewable leaders are able to understand how to continue to learn and grow rather than become stuck in a method or mindset that is inflexible.

Executive coaching concentrates on equipping, challenging and encouraging the executive. We also call it professional development since the goal is to help the executive develop their skills and talents to their maximum potential to carry out their profession as leaders.

Most who receive executive coaching are leaders of corporations, senior management, top salespeople or individuals who are leading government departments or ministries. Some are in professions like law, medicine or education, where their mandate includes effective leadership.

It is different from counseling in the sense that we are not looking at the life issues that are part of your personal history that might be holding you back. Nor do we do medical assessment. We do recommend that executives see their healthcare professionals regularly due to the stresses of leadership and the health risks that can be associated with those demands.

Coaching really looks forward in terms of where you are today and what will help you to achieve your goals. It means looking at the kinds of challenges that you are facing today and working through those in a way that is constructive and positive.

One of the illustrations we use is that of the old kings and queens. Monarchs were always better off when they had a sage nearby. For the executive, it does not hurt to have somebody beside you who can say, "Here are the things to think about." It can also be a time for questions or just a chance to reflect on your world.

That king-sage or queen-sage relationship is something that enhances the effectiveness of the leader.

Executive coaches understand the particular needs of people in leadership positions. When you are in a leadership position, you often feel alone. Sometimes that is by necessity because in order to lead, there has to be some separation. You will have to implement decisions that might not be popular because it is part of your responsibility to the organization. There is a benefit to having someone who is outside of the immediate situation to review the issues that you are confronting.

We deal with leaders at different stages of their story. Many people think that executive coaching means intervening when there is a crisis. Certainly, we deal with a lot of crises. Executive coaches frequently get called into situations in which there is a job change or a position is on the line. Occasionally there is the leader who lost their position and now must rethink where they go from here.

Often overlooked is the benefit of coaching during good times. It might be tempting to sail through the good times, but those are the times when you need to look at who you are and where you are going in making decisions that will help you to be prepared for the tough times that are to come. There are things that you should be doing in the good times that will help you weather those tough times that inevitably come as part of leadership.

In some cases, executive coaches are brought by human resources departments when executives are in a difficult or transitional stage at their organization. Coaches help to protect the company's investment in that leader by giving them the tools and support to succeed. HR can use coaching as a way to do some preventive medicine. Coaching allows an independent perspective to assess both the situation and the leader.

Good HR programs share this same objective with the executive coach. They want to help everybody who works for them to be successful and to make the company successful, and that is precisely the executive coach's goal.

CHOOSING AN EXECUTIVE COACH

How do you select an executive coach to give you the professional development that a great coach can give?

Start by looking for someone who is an executive coach vs. a life coach. Life coaches are very helpful in assisting anyone with the elements that lead to a satisfying life. Executive coaches have leaders only as the focus of their work.

Like most important service roles we hire, it must begin with the relationship. If your first impression is that the prospective coach does not have excellent interpersonal relationship skills, do not bother with all the excellent ideas and credentials that might be available. We can only be successfully coached by those we trust and respect. If you do not sense that they have the ability to relate to you effectively, you will never trust them with the wide range of business and life topics you will need to discuss.

Checking references and recommendations is helpful as you vet an executive coach.

In the final analysis, however, it really comes down to a coach with the personality style that works for you. They need to be someone committed to helping people rather than controlling them. Look for someone to be a positive influence in your life in the same way you want to be that for your team.

Beyond just the superficial "people skills" of being a talker; they need to be good listeners who are able to take in what is going on within the person. As good communicators, they can also share ideas in ways that are meaningful.

I also believe that the coach should be a friend. That surprises people, as we are conditioned to think of coaching like counseling, where you want someone who is objectively distant. But in coaching, you really want someone on your side who is there to take you as you are, where you are and help you move forward to succeed. Think of your best coaches in sports or your favorite teachers in school. You knew that they cared about you doing well and they wanted you to reach your potential. They were not the neutral arbiters who were merely measuring your ability to pass or fail the test.

Like all relationships, it is based on a growing trust in what also defines friendship. Find a coach who has perspective but who is also willing to commit to your success. You want someone who can have that kind of a fellowship approach where they step into the boat with you as opposed to calling instructions from the comfort of the shore.

This may seem too obvious to include, but it is too important to miss. Choose a coach who is going to be encouraging. We can never have enough encouragement in life, especially as executives. You never can get enough encouragement. A great coach will encourage and challenge you.

I also believe that the best executive coaching is for the whole person. There are many parts of our life that can stress or nurture us. Understanding how life outside the office comes to work with us each day and how the office goes home after work helps us recognize that we are more than our jobs. People with challenges at home will not have the same potential each day at work. Stresses at work will undermine our family life and health and will rob us of the full life we aspire to experience in the short time we are here.

I also believe that the spiritual dimension of life is very important. For some people, that is expressed in their faith experience rooted in a certain religious or philosophical background. For others it is less well defined. The spiritual dimension of life gives us the appreciation of beauty and wonder. It can be very important to renewing our creativity, energy, motivation, purpose and passion for life. Some people take advantage of that in the coaching process, and some people will not. As part of a commitment to coaching the whole person, a coach needs to be able to explore that with the leader if the executive wishes to do so.

One thing that people ask me is whether executive coaches have to have worked in a particular industry to be able to coach executives effectively in that field. That is not necessary since coaching is different from training or teaching. The technical or specific information relevant to the industry or area of service of the leader usually has little to do with the coaching process.

A great executive coach is one who will help you succeed no matter where you are or what you are doing through encouragement, trust and insight shared together. Choose an executive coach with those commitments and you will truly benefit from your time together.

SPEAK TO BE HEARD

Here is a bonus section that is especially helpful for leaders who struggle with public speaking. That is not the case for some people, so that is why we have included this as an extra section to support the leadership of those whom this would help.

Public speaking is one of the great fears that most people have. It is often expected that a leader will need to address a group of people either inside or outside of the organization. Here are some strategies that can make public speaking easier to minimize some of the stress and make you more effective.

The first thing when it comes to public speaking—the most important big idea—is to be you. You may say, "But I'm not a public speaker, so 'being me' is the wrong idea." The good news is that the best public speakers are people who are able to just be themselves. At some point, they gave themselves permission to just be who they are. You now officially have been granted that, too. It is okay to be you.

You do not have to be Winston Churchill, Ronald Reagan or Barack Obama. You do not have to be somebody who can use very long words and sound like a professor. You do not have to be somebody who is so relaxed and can do stand-up comedy. You do not have to be anything other than who you are. That is what engages the audience. That is what engages the people who are listening to you when they feel like they are really *listening* to you. Not somebody else, not a mimic, not an imitation of somebody, but really just listening to you. As a public speaker, that is your goal.

But there are some things to make you more effective in communicating your ideas. The following are some tips and tools to help you relax and feel more confident when you present.

You have a presentation that has certain content to it appropriate to the occasion or purpose of your presentation. How you can prepare the content that you need for your audience? You want to ensure that you know what information must be covered before the end of the speech. No one wants to have to do a follow-up memo to the speech with a list of things you meant to say. (Think awards ceremony thank-you list for inspiration!) Preparation of your content is one of the reasons that good speakers are able to relax. They already know what they are going to say.

Know how you are going to start your presentation and what you will do to finish it. In the rest of your content, it is a case of "How am I going to get there?" When drawing a map, you want to start at a certain place, and you want to finish at a certain place. The question then just becomes: How do we get from here to there? Having a clear, precise idea of the beginning and end helps.

Any presentation always involves the one and the many. We want everyone in the room to think that we are talking just to them at the same time we are talking to everyone. We do this by ensuring that everything we say could be understood by everyone in the meeting. If you use jargon or a technical term that not everyone would know, define it as you present. Outstanding presenters have perfected that ability to connect with each person even though there is a very diverse audience. Being aware of this helps. The presentation is a combination of the one and the many.

It applies to the illustrations you choose. Mention actor John Wayne to a group of 20-year-olds and they will not know who that is. That would be a poor choice of an illustration. If your audience has a wide range of interests or generations, use multiple illustrations so each person makes the connection. Illustrations make presentations memorable.

Remember the line "Sugar and spice and everything nice"? In your presentation, you want your content to include some sugar and some spice. The sweetness aspect is that you are communicating something as a real person and that you care about your audience. You want them to feel that they are worth your attention and that you are glad they are there.

The spice aspect is important, too. Spices, herbs, and flavors make a dinner memorable. Include content that has some spice to it for a different twist by adding creativity to your content. A list of ten items spoken in sequence does not a good speech make. Try to include some surprises and diversions to keep the audience engaged. Spice it up!

The next pair to remember is sun and snow. The idea here is that there are going to be some parts of your presentation that are bright and cheery and that make the audience go, "Ahh." Those are the emotional illustrations and words that warm up an audience. Then there are other parts of it that are more like the snow in that they are cold, hard facts that need to be communicated. You want to communicate in such a way that people feel good about your company and the things that you are doing. However, you also want to deal with the cold, hard facts and communicate them in such a way that they are not misunderstood.

Stories are very helpful in any kind of presentation. Find a story, a parable, or a saying that will transport your audience's imagination. Talk to that creative right side of the brain, not just the factual left side. Communicate with the heart. Remember how interesting the simple concept of "show and tell" was when you were younger? "Show and tell" still works for adults. If you can bring up some visual aids or something that they can look at, this can be very powerful. If you are giving a corporate presentation and you want to do something that involves a product, have the product there. Hold it up. Do the "show and tell" so that people have the opportunity to learn about it. All of those things help add a dimension to your presentation.

Next, think about the concepts of heavy and light. There are so many parts of the presentation that are just heavy. Balance the heavy with the light. When it needs to be heavy, give the heavy information. Be as clear and crisp as you can. Yet also remember the benefits of adding something a little lighter. One of the best ways to be light in a presentation is to make fun of yourself. While it might seem like fun to make fun of other people, it is very dangerous to do that because you can easily cross the line and offend someone who is not even the target. It is far better from your audience's perspective for you to make a joke about yourself. For example, you might say, "You know, I was looking at what I was going to wear today, and the good news that is I'm standing behind a podium, so you do not have to see all of the mismatched colors I would have chosen." Make a joke about yourself. It does not have to be something traumatic or dramatic. It just has to be a little something that allows the audience to relax with you and to feel good that you are a human being. Even though you are presenting very valuable and important information, it is not a bad thing for you to be able to chuckle about yourself and not take yourself too seriously. Great speakers have the ability to make fun of themselves in a light way that helps to balance the heavy stuff with the light stuff—and in the end, both sides become more effective.

Quick and clear is a couplet that is good for you to remember. In your presentations, be quick by using some shorter sentences. Having it short and quick is very powerful. Being clear in what you want to say is also important, because there is nothing worse than the audience sitting there in a fog of long sentences, saying, "Huh? What was that?" and "What did he say?" or "What did she mean?" Be so clear on the big idea that someone would be able to repeat it back to you if asked. That ensures that good communication has occurred.

Tears and fears is pair of words for a speaker to remember. Recognize that as your audience is sitting and listening to you, they are dealing with their own world, as well. As much as they may be sitting and engaged in every single word that you are saying, they are thinking about all of the things that are part of their world, like a list of things they need to do as soon as the meeting is over. Some are weighing the challenges they have. Maybe they have a conflict with the spouse, parents, or children. They have fears about today and their future. There are all of these other things that are going on in a person's mind, and it is very hard for them to be able to get that noise out of the way. One tactic is to include an emotional component to get their attention. If you do not engage their emotions, you will not be able to convey the content and the factual information.

Here are some techniques you can use to improve the delivery of your speech.

The first concept is to and fro. Good speakers are always looking at their audience. They recognize that the audience is there. To and fro means that I am going to be looking at the audience members on one side, and over the course of my presentation I am going to look at the audience members on the other side. You want to make eye contact with your group by going across. To and fro is going to give them a sense that you are really talking to them. You want to include your entire audience. You do not have to do it like a lighthouse where you are going around and around. It is almost as if you are saying, "I'm going to be looking at you soon, so pay attention."

Another aspect of the presentation is deep and shallow. In deep and shallow, much like to and fro, it has to do with your audience. Deep and shallow addresses the front and back of the audience. We have people who are up close, the shallow. Then we have the deeper part of our audience, way in the back. We want to make eye contact with the people who are in front of us as well as the people who are way in the distance.

Fast and slow is another key pair of words for your presentation. If you always speak at the same pace and the same words come out the same way, the audience will fall asleep. Fast and slow means that you need to vary the speed at which you speak. There are some points that you want to make very dramatically. Other points are where you need to slow down so that people understand that this is the most significant part of the whole evening. By going faster and going slower, by varying your speed, this also will help people to recognize the content. Slow down when it is an important point. Speed it up when you want them to have more energy.

Then there is the concept of high and low. High and low tones are good thing to have in your voice. There are times when you want to raise your voice; you want to go high with your voice because you want to create a question. If you want to ask a question, "Could this be the end of Flash Gordon?" you go up at the end. "We knew that this was going to be the worst of all possible times" would have your tone go down. So, sometimes you are high and other times you are low, but your audience will always be engaged.

The next part is the method is plant and grow. When you are making a presentation, sometimes you have a new idea, concept, or information to share. You are planting a seed. Plant that seed early on so there is time to grow it over the course of your presentation. As you return to the idea in your presentation and add additional information or perspectives with it, the idea will start to take root and grow in the minds of your audience. Give them an opportunity to start to engage it.

The last point brings us back to where we began. Any presentation is only going to be as good as it allows you to be you. Be well-prepared. Do the things that will make you more effective. In your preparation, have someone listen to you if you are not comfortable yet doing speeches. You may want to get some helpful feedback. It also gives you an estimate of how long your presentation will take in case it needs to be shorter. (No one really wants a longer speech!)

Allow your uniqueness to come out in your presentation. Remember, most people sitting in any audience feel exactly like you do. They are saying, "I'm glad it's her" or "I'm glad it's him that's up there and not me." They feel the same way.

So, just relax. Treat the audience members as friends. You will become more like yourself, and that is a very good thing.

USEFUL LINKS AND CONTACTS

Strategic Seminars - Workshops and seminars for corporations and groups covering topics on business, health, leadership, motivation, relationships, team building, customer service, and more. We are flexible to help corporations and groups of all sizes and with different budgets. There is a special focus on leadership and group development services for corporations. Seminars are offered in the U.S., Canada and the Caribbean. Contact us in Chicago or Toronto.

www.strategic-seminars.com

Canadian Executive Coaching - Executive coaching for Canadian senior executives, managers, department heads, top salespeople and leaders. Serving a wide range of industry, government and not-for-profit entities with one-on-one coaching to improve performance and provide personal support and reflection. Based on a whole-person model that recognizes our different skills, passions and abilities, Canadian Executive Coaching will help you reach your full potential as a leader and as a person. Member of the Fellowship of Executive Coaches.

www.canadian-executive-coaching.com

Harcote Industries – Harcote provides marketing, consulting and distribution services for corporations. There is a special interest and expertise in assisting start-up ventures.

www.harcote.com

Dr. Blair Lamb, M.D. – The Lamb Clinic is a research and treatment center for the understanding and treatment of pain conditions affecting people of all ages. It has a special focus on fibromyalgia, migraines, arthritis, whiplash, and more. Extensive articles are included on a range of pain topics.

www.drlamb.com

Learn about featured seminar speaker Dr. Larry Komer, M.D., with his innovative research and treatments using hormone therapy as part of an overall wellness and anti-aging strategy for men, women and those who have been injured. Excellent information is available on the website for women, covering such topics as menopause, bio-identical hormone therapies, breast cancer and more. For men, you can learn about andropause, testosterone, fitness and the various conditions affecting men. New understanding on traumatic brain injury is part of his research, as well.

www.drkomer.com

www.mastersmensclinic.com.

Palantir Publishing is the publisher of Grant D. Fairley's Look Up – Way Up! The Friendly Giant. This book is the biography of television's beloved The Friendly Giant – Robert M. Homme.

www.palantir-publishing.com

Silverwoods Publishing is the publisher of the book *Up to the Cottage – Memories of Muskoka*, which describes the joys and memories of simple cottages in the golden era of Muskoka. Grant D. Fairley recalls the heartwarming stories typical of life at cottages in the second half of the 20th Century. Whether you spent time in Muskoka, Haliburton, the Kawarthas or another place where cottages and cabins were your home away from home, this book is for you.

www.silverwoods-publishing.com

York Downs Pharmacy – Toronto-based pharmacy with advanced compounding as well as other educational and health products and services shipping across Canada.

www.yorkdownsrx.com

FOR FURTHER INVESTIGATION

Here are some books that are worth reading on different aspects of being an effective leader.

- *Blink: The Power of Thinking Without Thinking* by Malcolm Gladwell
- *Finding Your Element: How to Discover Your Talents and Passions and Transform Your Life* by Ken Robinson
- *How Will You Measure Your Life?* by Clayton M Christensen
- *Outliers: The Story of Success* by Malcolm Gladwell
- *Quiet: The Power of Introverts in a World That Can't Stop Talking* by Susan Cain
- *Own Your Future: Wisdom for Wealth and a Better Tomorrow* by Grant D. Fairley & Michael H. Lanthier
- *Rumsfeld's Rules* by Donald Rumsfeld
- *The Effective Executive: The Definitive Guide to Getting the Right Things Done* by Peter F Drucker
- *The Element: How Finding Your Passion Changes Everything* by Ken Robinson
- *The Great Degeneration: How Institutions Decay and Economies Die* by Niall Ferguson

- *The Mobile Wave: How Mobile Intelligence Will Change Everything by Michael Saylor*
- *The Power of Habit: Why We Do What We Do and How to Change It by Charles Duhigg*
- *The Social Animal: The Hidden Sources of Love, Character, and Achievement by David Brooks*
- *The Tools: Transform Your Problems into Courage, Confidence, and Creativity by Phil Stutz and Barry Michels*
- *The Tipping Point: How Little Things Can Make a Big Difference by Malcolm Gladwell*
- *Thinking, Fast and Slow by Daniel Kahneman*

POSTSCRIPT

Who Am I?

Archetypes go back a long way in many religious and philisophical traditions. These have been organized by different people along the way including Plato and Jung (Collected Works of C.G. Jung, Volume 9 (Part 1): Archetypes and the Collective Unconscious by C. G. Jung) among many others. I like the list from The 12 Common Archetypes referenced by Carl Golden and also found in books by Carol S. Pearson like "The Hero Within" from 1998. Some of those who write about this suggest that all of us have all of the twelve archetypes within us. They explore how to engage each aspect of this or follow a progression of the archetypes as a form of passages for each person to experience. I think a simpler observation is that we probably have one or maybe two of the archetypes that are most apparent in us. Perhaps as we age, there is a mellowing that can make a hero into a sage but the heroic Churchill was 65 when he became prime minister. David was never Solomon nor vis versa. As with spiritual gifts, we may do and should be all things but we probably are best in one or two areas of service. Many talented and exceptional people struggle not with what they could do but what they will do. I have met many individuals who may have chosen widely different careers based on their intellectual capacity. This is where passion also plays a role in connecting us to a meaningful career or a best of many good choices.

Conductors and Captains

If you have not seen the A&E Hornblower TV (now DVD) series, it is a great adventure. You will see some wonderful leadership training, skill development and mentoring in the series. It is especially true of Horatio Hornblower learning from his captains Keane and Pellew. I like the Richard Sharpe series for that kind of leadership learned in the field experiences.

The Real Deal

I have always been enchanted by Churchill's story. It is one that includes the ups and downs that are so characteristic of great leaders. As someone who believes in both purpose and destiny, I like how Churchill is one of many leaders who illustrate the power of when the times and the leader finally are in synch. I also dropped a note about Charles Frederick Williams at that point since Churchill followed along the trail blazed by Williams and others of the Victoria age of Empire in Great Britain. Charles Williams was my great-great-grandfather.

Arts and Sciences

It was my privilege to not only watch Donald MacDonald's leadership while I was growing up but I had the privilege of working with him on the use of ViaVoice. He is a charming and remarkable man who made his mark as a leader.

Did You Bring the Playbook?

At the time of writing, the incredible Gareth Bale is rumored to be on the transfer block with perhaps Real Madrid. It would be a great loss for Tottenham and the English Premier League but the price tag would no doubt give Spurs some comfort. A salute to EA Sports™ in their early FIFA games. Whatever scouting formulations they used were quite amazing in projecting the development of a number of talented players. Most striking to my son Doug and myself was Gareth Bale. When we were playing in the mid-2000s, the game included not just the top players but the many who were on the bench or reserves like the very young Gareth Bale. In the game, you could play multiple seasons. Through this, you would watch players age to maturity or later to retirement. We observed this remarkable Gareth Bale in some of the games that projected what players would be like in 2010 and beyond. Even though his stated position was left-back, we began to use him as a winger and sometimes a center. His play became a wild-card that made our games not only more enjoyable but improved our winning percentage. Credit to EA Sports in their ability to see his potential. It is impressive.

On a Swing or on Fire?

This section references the thinking of Diana Baumrind's parenting styles in 1966 that were expanded by E.E. Maccoby and J.A. Martin in 1983. Obviously parenting and leadership are different roles however the human responses to authority are conditioned by our early experiences. Children and adults continue to share many characteristic patterns. While it is a parents responsibility to control as well as support children (changing from control to influence as they grow up), I do not advocate leaders controlling the behavior of those they lead except in times of crisis or emergency where authority needs to be exercised decisively for public safety and the common good.

Exit Stage Right

This chapter references the book, "To Resist or to Surrender?" by Paul Tournier

ABOUT THE AUTHOR

Grant D. Fairley is a principal speaker with Strategic Seminars, a division of McK Consulting Inc. His seminars cover a wide range of topics, including leadership, finance, team building, sales training, relationships, personal development, motivation, and more.

He is also an executive coach working with corporate and government leaders and senior sales professionals to enhance and develop their careers and personal effectiveness.

Grant is a graduate of Wheaton College, Wheaton, Illinois.

Over the years, he has had a liberal arts life with a range of activities that include teaching, writing and encouraging as common threads in the many roles.

His recent books include *Look Up – Way Up! The Friendly Giant*, the biography of Robert Homme, and *Up to the Cottage – Memories of Muskoka*, a book about the love of old cottages and cottage life in the 1900s.

He co-authored with his friend and colleague, Michael H. Lanthier, *Own Your Future – Wisdom for Wealth and a Better Tomorrow*. This book introduces readers to the big ideas of personal investment and career planning. It is also helpful for perspectives on how to build wealth for the long term while making wise decisions along the way. Grant's next book includes his unique perspectives on the classic fairy tales and fables is *Enchanted Living - Insights for Your Life from Fairy Tales & Fables*. With the retelling of the traditional stories, Grant finds a new perspective with an application to life and business. These fairy tales have been a popular part of his seminar presentations over the past few years. Another upcoming book looks at the baby-boomer generation as it enters the retirement years. Co-authored with geriatric psychiatrist and friend, Dr. William S. Cook, MD this book is entitled, *What's Left in Your Box? A Baby Boomer's Guide to Finishing Well*. This book explores the challenges of facing retirement and the aging process. The focus is on the opportunity to do a reset of your life to make the golden years not only enjoyable but meaningful as well.

In addition to writing books, he is the co-author of a number of patents relating to technology and healthcare.

Most days, he is sharing with others through seminars, workshops and retreats. Some of his seminars are available on YouTube www.youtube.com/

strategicseminar. You can hear his podcast chats online about his business and life seminar topics on the BlogTalk Radio channel www.blogtalkradio.com/strategic-seminars

Grant serves as an executive coach providing support and perspectives to senior executives in business, government, sales and other organizations. His podcast chats online about executive coaching on the BlogTalk Radio channel www.blogtalkradio.com/vip-coach

He is especially delighted to serve in his local church.

He continues to learn and grow through his relationship with his wife Cari, the children, the family and friends who are in his story. For these gifts and so much more, he is very grateful.

Grant would welcome your comments on the book. You may contact him at fairley@silverwoods-publishing.com

Follow Grant on Twitter @grantfairley www.twitter.com/grantfairley

His Tumblr blog is called Ship to Shore under the pen name of one of his ancestors, Admiral Wood http://admiralwood.tumblr.com

Silverwoods Publishing